Once Upon a Time

CAMBRIDGE HANDBOOKS FOR LANGUAGE TEACHERS
General Editor: Michael Swan

This is a series of practical guides for teachers of English and other
languages. Illustrative examples are usually drawn from the field of English
as a foreign or second language, but the ideas and techniques described can
equally well be used in the teaching of any language.

In this series:

Drama Techniques in Language Learning – A resource book of
communication activities for language teachers
by Alan Maley and Alan Duff

Games for Language Learning
by Andrew Wright, David Betteridge and Michael Buckby

Discussions that Work – Task-centred fluency practice *by Penny Ur*

Once Upon a Time – Using stories in the language classroom
by John Morgan and Mario Rinvolucri

Teaching Listening Comprehension *by Penny Ur*

Keep Talking – Communicative fluency activities for language teaching
by Friederike Klippel

Working with Words – A guide to teaching and learning vocabulary
by Ruth Gairns and Stuart Redman

Learner English – A teacher's guide to interference and other problems
edited by Michael Swan and Bernard Smith

Testing Spoken Language – A handbook of oral testing techniques
by Nic Underhill

Literature in the Language Classroom – A resource book of ideas and
activities *by Joanne Collie and Stephen Slater*

Dictation – New methods, new possibilities
by Paul Davis and Mario Rinvolucri

Grammar Practice Activities – A practical guide for teachers *by Penny Ur*

Testing for Language Teachers *by Arthur Hughes*

The Inward Ear – Poetry in the language classroom
by Alan Maley and Alan Duff

Pictures for Language Learning *by Andrew Wright*

Five-Minute Activities – A resource book of short activities
by Penny Ur and Andrew Wright

Once Upon a Time

Using stories in the language classroom

*John Morgan
and Mario Rinvolucri*

CAMBRIDGE
UNIVERSITY PRESS

Published by the Press Syndicate of the University of Cambridge
The Pitt Building, Trumpington Street, Cambridge CB2 1RP
40 West 20th Street, New York, NY 10011–4211, USA
10 Stamford Road, Oakleigh, Melbourne 3166, Australia

First published 1983
Ninth printing 1992

Printed in Great Britain
at The Bath Press, Avon

Library of Congress catalogue card number: 83–5356

British Library cataloguing in publication data

Morgan, John

Once upon a time – (Cambridge handbooks for
language teachers)
1. English language – Study and teaching –
Foreign students
I. Title   II. Rinvolucri, Mario
428.2'4'091   PE1128

ISBN 0 521 25269 5   hard covers
ISBN 0 521 27262 9   paperback

Once Upon a Time was originally published in pilot form by Pilgrims
Publications, Canterbury, England. This Cambridge University Press edition
has been extensively revised and expanded.

MX

Contents

Thanks

We wish to thank the following people:

Students with whom we have learnt to tell stories.

Both sceptical and enthusiastic colleagues, in particular Jane Lockwood, Katya Benjamin, Paul Davis, Mo Strangeman, Cynthia Beresford, Jan Aspeslagh, Charles Williams, James Dixey, Michael Swan, Margaret Callow, Carlos Maeztu, Richard and Marjorie Baudins, Elena Morgan, Lindsay Brown, Loren McGrail, Sarah Braine.

Bernard Dufeu who opened our eyes to the psychodrama use of tales.

The artistic oral tradition we know best is that of the Greek shadow puppeteers and we particularly want to acknowledge the insights gained from working with Giorgos Charidimos.

Books that have helped us in our thinking about the oral story include:
Bruno Bettelheim, *The Uses of Enchantment*, Pengüin 1978
Iona and Peter Opie, *The Classic Fairy Tales*, OUP 1974
Vladimir Propp, *Morphology of the Folktale*, Austin 1968
Gianni Rodari, *Grammatica della Fantasia*, Einaudi 1973

Finally, this book owes a heavy debt to the various oral traditions of which it is a curious continuation, and to individuals whose written stories we have 'skeletonised' in preparation for many oral tellings.

J.M.
M.R.

To the teacher

Among both practising language teachers and applied linguists there is an increasing awareness that successful second-language learning is far more a matter of unconscious acquisition than of conscious, systematic study. Stephen Krashen (*Second Language Acquisition and Second Language Learning*, Pergamon 1981) goes so far as to say that 'the major function of the second-language classroom is to provide intake for acquisition'.

It is our view that the 'intake' required to facilitate language acquisition will be very different from the materials currently provided in the classroom as part of systematic structural or notional courses. If unconscious processes are to be enlisted, then the whole person will need to be engaged: we shall no longer be able to rely on the learner's general 'motivation' or on the intrinsic charms of the target language to sustain him or her through the years of monotonous drilling and bland role-play. Classroom activities will have to be structured to serve immediate rather than long-term needs, to promote rather than practise communication and expression.

This book is offered as a step in that direction. Within the frame of storytelling–that most ancient and compelling of human activities–we propose a wide range of classroom exercises and more than 70 story outlines ('skeletons') for you and your students to work from. The exercises range from introspective to highly interactive; from beginner to advanced; many are offered as communicative alternatives to traditional language-teaching activities; all, we hope, are engaging and rewarding in themselves.

'I CAN'T TELL STORIES' You could be right, but if so you're in a small minority. In our experience very few teachers of English can *read aloud* adequately, but almost all have a hidden talent as story-tellers. Section 1 suggests ways in which you can work from a bare outline to an adequate and even 'magic' telling.

LISTENING COMPREHENSION The quality of listening that takes place when you tell your class a story (provided you tell rather than read aloud) is radically different from that during conventional

1

listening comprehension from tape. The latter is always third-person listening, a kind of eavesdropping that is strangely uncompelling. To be told a story by a live storyteller, on the contrary, involves one in 'I–thou' listening, where the listeners can directly influence the telling. Even if you are a non-native teacher of English, the communicative gain will more than outweigh the 'un-Englishness' you may hear in your telling.

FOLLOWING UP A STORY 'Comprehension questions' and paraphrase exercises are standard classroom follow-ups to listening work: after a story they at best dilute, at worst destroy, its effect on the listener. In Section 2 you will find a variety of alternative follow-up exercises. 2.1, for example, gives the student an opportunity to decide for himself or herself which questions (if any) he or she wants answered, and to hear the answers from a classmate. 2.4 uses role-assignment to explore the group's feelings towards characters in a story; 2.14 uses a drawing exercise to help students 'cap' one story with another. All the exercises encourage the recycling of new language.

RETELLING Being required to retell a story to someone who has just heard it is a pleasure few of us would willingly repeat: yet this is often what we force upon our students. Section 3 suggests activities in which retelling is both necessary and enjoyable.

STORIES AND GRAMMAR Many traditional stories abound in powerful repeated phrases (e.g. 'Who's been sleeping in MY bed?'). For elementary and intermediate students, such stories (suitably chosen) can be used as an almost subliminal grammar input. 4.1 gives some examples of this.

It is also a fairly simple matter to angle your telling and/or follow-up exercises in such a way that particular structures are demanded of the student: from common strong verbs to third conditionals.

In Section 8 you are introduced to the Silent Way reduction technique which has the students working intensively on grammar, syntax, intonation and meaning all at the same time. After 20 minutes intensive work the story they started out from has vanished!

FROM LISTENING TO ORAL PRODUCTION In Section 5 we suggest ways of collaborating with students in the production of stories: 5.2 shows a narrator plus Greek chorus technique; 5.8

shows the teacher modelling vocabulary from *within* a group; in 5.1 a use is found for the language laboratory.

ORAL PRODUCTION There are stories hidden inside everyone. Elementary students will bring them out in dramatic, excited half-sentences; advanced speakers will reach out for ever more vivid or exact expression. For all, adequate communication is an attainable miracle, if the teacher is prepared to allow it. Section 6 provides frames for the recall or creation of students' own stories; Section 7 goes a little deeper–into one's real or imaginary past.

PICTURE STORIES We are all familiar with the 'picture story' as a device for provoking narrative work. Unfortunately, anyone with normal eyesight produces much the same story, which robs the telling of any point. In 6.9 we provide symbolic pictures to provoke a wide range of different stories. Once they have created their own story, students are keen to tell them and to find out what others have made of the 'doodlestrip':

STORY POOL At the end of the book you will find twenty story outlines to supplement those scattered through the exercises. We have tried to make these as varied as possible, but recognise that we cannot span the range of tastes of all the possible readers of this book. If you find pleasure and profit in telling stories with your class, then we hope you will be able to add your own stories to the pool.

FAIRY STORIES We have consciously included a number of fairy stories in the book: we feel these are suitable for work with both very young learners and with adults, but they are perhaps not a good bet in most classes of adolescents. In this age group we suggest you concentrate on symbolic, literary, and problem stories.

There are, however, great advantages to working on fairy stories with older people. They are often familiar in outline (though seldom

3

in detail) in the student's mother tongue; the language is simple yet the meanings are evocative and many-layered; and the stories bring back, often in a flood of excitement, memories of one's own childhood and that of one's children.

Section 1 Telling a story

One day, while testing material for this book, we decided to tell the same story in each of the two groups of students we were working with, and to record ourselves while doing so. The story, a Ghanaian folk tale, goes like this:

> A hunchback girl protects her father's beans from wild animals
> In the fields, she is visited by fairies
> They ask her for bean soup
> She says she can't bend down to pick the beans, because of her hump
> The fairies remove the hump
> She picks the beans and cooks them
> The fairies eat, thank her
> They replace the hump and leave
> Her father tells her: 'You silly girl, you should have run away before they could replace the hump'
> Next day, the same thing. She runs off before they replace the hump
> She hides in the hut from the fairies
> A week later there is a dance in the village
> She can't resist—joins the dance
> While dancing, she feels a weight on her shoulders
> She turns, sees the fairies leaving the village
>
> (from *Folk Tales and Fables*, ed. P. Itayemi & P. Gurrey)

In one room the students heard:

> There was a farmer / in the north of the country / who was very poor / and he just had a couple of fields where he grew yams and beans and things / and he lived by himself with his daughter / and every day he would go out to his fields and dig / plant his yams / look after his farm / his daughter would go / out with him / but she had a hump on her back she was a hunchback and she couldn't do any real work she couldn't bend / and her job was to go to the more distant field and / just guard the beans from the monkeys /

5

who would come down from the forest around   /   one day she
went out to the field   /   and   /   while she was there some
fairies came out of the wood   /   and asked her for   /
beans   /   they wanted her to cook them   /   and make them   /
a meal   /   she said she couldn't because she couldn't bend to
pick the beans   /   so one of the fairies came up to her put his
hand on her back and lifted the hump off her back   /   and said
now you can pick beans   /   well she did this she picked the
beans and she put them in a pot made a fire cooked the beans
and gave them to the fairies   /   and they ate them thanked her
for them   /   and turned to go and as they left they replaced the
hump on her back   /   When she came back to the hut she told
her father what had happened and her father said now if they
come again   /   and they probably will   /   when they take the
hump off your back   /   don't go and pick the beans run away
and hide   /   then you'll grow up straight   /   like the
other girls   /   so the next day she went out to the field and the
fairies did come and asked her for beans   /   and took the hump
off her back   /   and instead of going   /   out into the field
to pick the beans   /   she turned and ran   /   as fast as she
could   /   she rushed back to the village and hid in the hut   /
that evening when her father came home   /   he advised
her to stay in the house   /   because the fairies now would be
looking for her   /   but after a few weeks he thought they
would go away   /   so she stayed in the house   /   for a
week   /   and   /   then there was a festival in the village   /
and all the girls went out into the streets of the village   /   and
they danced   /   and the girl looked   /   out of her window at
the girls   /   in   /   their bright   /   costumes   /   dancing in
the street   /   and she couldn't resist it   /   she'd always loved
dancing and she'd never been able to dance and now she
could   /   and out into the street she went   /   danced with the
other girls   /   while she was dancing   /   she felt a weight   /
on her shoulders   /   turned round   /   and there she saw the
fairies   /   quietly   /   going off   /   out of the village

In the other room the students heard:

Once upon a time there was a village   /   on the edge of a
desert   /   in the village there lived a man who had seven sons
he also had one daughter   /   his sons were straight and
upright   /   but his daughter   /   well   /   she had a hump on
her back   /   and she had to walk bent over   /   and this made
the man very very unhappy   /   and it made the girl very very
unhappy   /   she couldn't pick things up   /   she couldn't
walk   /   properly   /   and she couldn't dance   /   the man

had a beanfield on the edge of the desert   /   and one of the
daughter's jobs was to go and watch the beanfield   /   and
make sure no animals or people stole beans from it   /   one
evening she was there   /   as night was falling   /   in this part
of the world night falls quickly   /   and as she was preparing to
go home suddenly some fairies appeared on the edge of the beanfield   /   and they came over   /   and one of them said to her
/   we're hungry   /   pick us some beans and make us a bean
soup   /   but the girl looked at them sadly   /   and said   /   I
can't bend down to pick the beans   /   but the fairy   /   came
close behind her and lifted   /   the hump from off her back   /
and she could stand upright and walk straight   /   she smiled
/   and began to pick beans   /   she made a fire   /   and she
made the fairies a bean soup   /   which they ate greedily
/   and then disappeared   /   across the edge of the field back   /
into the desert   /   and the girl   /   ran home   /   but as
she was running   /   suddenly   /   she felt the hump   /   coming back onto her shoulders   /   and by the time she got home
she was stooped forward   /   and could only walk slowly   /
and she told her father everything that had happened   /   and
her father said to her   /   you acted wrong my daughter   /   you
should have run away as soon as the fairies took the hump off
your back   /   they couldn't have found you to put it back on
again   /   I'm sure they'll come back tomorrow   /   when it
happens run away   /   before they can put the hump back on
your shoulders   /   and so the next evening   /   the girl went to
the beanfield again and sure enough the fairies   /   appeared
over the edge of the field   /   and they asked her to make them a
bean soup again   /   and a fairy lifted the hump from off her
back   /   and quickly she ran out of the field and ran back
home to the village   /   she hid in her father's house   /   and
she could walk straight   /   and she realised that she could
dance   /   for that evening there was going to be a dance   /   at
the house of some neighbours where there was a wedding   /
and she   /   later on in the evening she crept out   /   and
went to the house   /   to the neighbour's house   /   and joined
the dancing   /   and then she saw   /   on the edge of the   /
dancing people   /   the fairies   /   suddenly   /   her hump was
there on her back again   /   she stooped forward   /   she could
dance no more

Telling not reading

The two versions not only differ from each other in both content
and language, but also in pace; and both differ from a story *reading*

in numerous ways. One can readily imagine the wide range of factors that might go to producing such differences: the mood of the teller when he or she first encountered the story; his or her mood while telling; the background experiences that lead, for example, to one teller seeing forest where the other saw desert landscape; the number and seating of the audience; the teller's relationship to the audience; and so on and so on. And these differences are in turn reflected in the language: sometimes fluent, sometimes hesitant and uncertain, broken by irregular pauses, but always definitely *spoken* language, the language of personal communication that is so often absent from the foreign-language classroom.

In some ways telling is easier than reading aloud: the reader may be forced to interpret speech patterns and rhythms very different from his or her own; he or she is forced to become aware of things normally taken for granted, such as breathing; and these technical problems may become a barrier between him or her and the author just as the book he or she is holding may become a physical barrier between him or her and his or her audience. In telling, on the other hand, one can shape the story to one's own needs, and while this may require the development of certain, perhaps buried, skills, the advantages are very great. In the first place, one can address one's audience directly: one can make eye contact or not as and when one chooses, use gesture and mime freely, expand or modify the form of one's telling as the occasion demands, and in general establish and maintain a community of attention between teller and listener.

Again, from the learner's point of view, it is of immense benefit to witness the process of framing ideas in the target language without, as in conversation, constantly having to engage in that process oneself: forcing students always to hear polished speech (or, worse, the bland monotony of specially constructed oral texts) does them a great disservice.

Since first starting to work with stories, we have come to realise something of the extent to which narrative underlies our conversational encounters with others, and of the deep need that people have to tell and exchange stories. We have also learned something about the ways in which storytelling can take place in the foreign-language classroom.

Finding and choosing stories

Stories are everywhere: in selecting for this book we have drawn on traditional fairy stories, folk tale collections, newspaper reports, literary short stories, films and plays, personal anecdotes, rumours, stories from our own childhood and from the childhood of our friends, students and colleagues, and on our own imagination. We have learned stories from our children and their friends, and from professionals like Propp and Rodari.

In selecting stories for the classroom, we have been guided by two main criteria: is this a story that *we* would enjoy telling and is this a story *our students* might find entertaining or thought-provoking? We have seldom been influenced by purely linguistic considerations in our choice (though this does play a part–see 4.1), and we have never allowed the language of an original text to determine suitability–indeed, many of the stories we have used have been taken from originals in languages other than English.

Making skeletons

We found early on that a brief written outline ('skeleton') provided the best way for us to store material for storytelling. The skeleton should give, in minimal form, a plot outline, background information where necessary (e.g. cultural context if the plot is heavily dependent on this), and a certain amount of character detail. There is no obligation to produce a continuous text–indeed, this could be an obstacle to improvisation–or to observe the conventions of punctuation and 'complete sentences'. The aim should be to record all those elements that are essential to the story, but only these. (The decision about what is essential is entirely, and rightly, subjective: faithfulness to an original text or to a 'writer's intention' play no part in this work.)

All the stories presented in this book are given in the form of skeletons. These are printed exactly as we would use them ourselves, and we have not attempted to provide a 'standardised form'. We think they will be at least adequate as they stand, and are sure that teachers who wish to work from their own material, and thus produce their own story skeletons, will develop their own style and technique. It must be emphasised that the skeleton merely provides the bare frame of the story for the teller to work from, and must not be referred to *during* a telling.

Preparing to tell

In preparing to tell a story, we have worked directly from skeletons. This has the effect both of distancing the teller from the rhythms and forms of the source (whether oral or written) and of focussing on what is essential to memorise—the plot and development. Except where formulaic expressions are essential to the story (e.g. in fairy stories such repetitions as 'What big..... you have, grandmother') we have consciously avoided all memorisation or recording of *forms of words*, concentrating on plot line and pace, and on 'getting the feel' of the story. A dress rehearsal, for example, in front of the mirror, may at times be helpful, but can easily lead to loss of involvement, and thus, in the classroom, failure to communicate; one rehearsal technique which gets round this is to replay the story in one's head while mumbling the rhythms of the story (but not the actual words of the telling) aloud. We have also found that a brief period of total relaxation before telling is of immense help.

Styles of storytelling

There are many ways of telling a story. One can unroll one's mat under the nearest tree and call together a crowd; one can buttonhole a stranger in a railway carriage or bar; one can murmur in the ear of a sleepy child. These and many other traditional modes of telling can have their counterparts in the foreign-language classroom. Standing, or sitting on a raised chair in front of rows of students one can capture something of the one-man theatre show, and aim to fire emotions or entertain by pure acting skill. In total contrast to this, sitting with the students, in a tight circle, can conjure memories of childhood storytelling. By seeking and exchanging eye contact, one can draw the students into the story, and give a sense of participation in the process of telling; withholding eye contact, on the other hand, can be used to increase the mood of fantasy, and to encourage introspection. Body posture, voice level, and variation in the external environment (furniture, lighting, colour) can also be made to heighten particular effects. Particular stories, and particular groups of listeners, will call for different styles of telling, and the teller should be aware of the range of possibility open to him or her. A certain amount of deliberate experimentation is very helpful to anyone trying to develop his or her own styles: see what happens, for example, if stories are told from behind the listeners, or with the whole group lying down.

The listener

Just as there are styles of telling, so there are styles of listening.
People do not always listen in the same way, or for the same end; nor
do all people listen for the ends we might want to prescribe. When,
for example, the schoolmaster punishes a child for 'daydreaming'
instead of 'paying attention' to what is being said, he is assuming
that the aim of the child's listening is the absorption and retention of
the story or argument. Thus, if the child fails to pay attention, the
worth of the telling, and by implication of the teller, is called into
question. In practice, quite the opposite may be the case: the telling
may be so powerful or stimulating that it sets up dominant trains of
thought in the listener's head which force the attention away from
the teller and along new and exciting paths. The storyteller should
not merely recognise that this, too, might be a valid aim, but take
steps to encourage and exploit it by, for example, allowing thinking
time within the telling, and by encouraging the listeners to share
their thoughts afterwards. Foreign learners may have their own,
special aims in listening: they may be concentrating on the structures
or rhythms of speech, and allow 'meanings' to pass them by; they
may be engaged in a range of translation processes; they may,
especially if they are advanced students, be making conscious attempts
to find, in the style of telling, models for things they themselves wish
to express—things which may be quite remote (for others) from the
story being told. This too the teller should be content with.

What not to do

There are no recipes for storytelling, but there are very clearly things
one should NOT do:
Don't tell stories you don't like, or are out of sympathy with.
Don't rate the story above the listener: tell the story for the sake of
      the listener, not for the sake of the story.
Don't become preoccupied with 'getting the language right'—your
      telling will become nervous or flat.
Don't tell from notes.

A skeleton

Here is an example of the story skeletons presented in the book.

The river

Summer
They reached the river, had been at war three years
Lull in fighting
Three of them went bathing—three shots
HQ put river out of bounds

He crept through wood to river bank
Propped rifle against tree, undressed, swam
Water cool and clean
Caught branch in midstream
Saw head in water. Ours? Theirs?
Head went to other bank

He swam back to rifle, got there first
Aimed at other climbing out of water
Could not squeeze trigger
Let rifle fall
Saw birds rise as shot rang out
His face hit the ground

(after Antonis Samarakis, *Zitite Elpis*)

Section 2   Stories and follow-ups

2.1   Revenge questions

Skeleton

The inventor

Inventor
Lived in country
Drew plans, tore them up, started again
For 40 years never spoke, read newspaper, or received
   letter
Didn't know radio existed

One day realised he had made invention
Day and night checked plans, calculations
He went to town

Cars instead of horses; electric instead of steam trains;
   escalators, refrigerators.
Quickly understood—saw telephone and said: 'Aha'
Told people in street 'I have made a great invention'
They did not care

He entered a cafe and explained to a man
'I have invented a machine which shows what's going on
   miles away'
'Oh the television—there's one in the corner—shall I turn
   it on?'

The inventor went home
At desk for a month—re-invented car
Same with escalator, telephone, refrigerator
The really hard thing is to invent things that already exist

(after Peter Bichsel, 'Der Erfinder', in *Kindergeschichten*)

Stories and follow-ups

Before class

Make one copy of the questions given below. On this copy add
the names of two people from your class in the blanks in questions 4
and 25. Then copy the number of sheets you will need for your class.

In class

1 Tell the students the story.
2 Give them the 'comprehension' questions below and invite them
   to *cross out* any they don't like or think are stupid. Each student
   should work on his or her own doing this. You are here inviting
   the student to take revenge on boring comprehension questions.
3 When students have read all the questions and crossed out those
   they want to, ask them to work in pairs and put to a partner the
   questions they have retained. Pair students who have retained a
   lot of questions with ones who have crossed out most or all of the
   questions.
4 Have them re-pair and repeat 3 above.

QUESTIONS

1   What did the man in the cafe tell his wife when he got home that
    night?
2   Is it deeply useful to invent things that have already been
    invented?
3   What did the inventor look like?
4   Did .... in this group like this story?
5   What kind of house did the inventor live in?
6   What is the underlying theme of this story, for you?
7   Where did the inventor get his living from?
8   Why did the inventor no longer know how to speak to people?
9   What new things surprised the inventor when he went into
    town?
10 Do *you* know anybody like this man?
11 What colour were the walls of the inventor's room?
12 Would your brother like this story?
13 What did the inventor look like?
14 What kind of father would the inventor make?
15 Why did the inventor finally decide to go into town?
16 What sort of town did you imagine as you listened to the story?
17 Was the inventor an anti-social man?

14

18 If the inventor was a Muslim, how many wives would he have?
19 In what ways, if any, do you sympathise with the inventor?
20 What did the inventor do in the trams?
21 Why did the inventor get angry in the cafe?
22 Was this man a lunatic?
23 How did the story begin?
24 Did the story happen for you in England, your own country or somewhere else?
25 Did .... in this group like the story?
26 What was the inventor's reaction to the new things he saw in the town?
27 Which of the new things did he probably find most revolutionary?
28 Why did this man want to invent things?
29 How did the story end?
30 Were there any roses in the inventor's garden?
31 If the inventor had had hobbies, what might they have been?
32 What sort of relationship do you imagine the inventor having had with his parents?
33 What did the man in the cafe offer to do for the inventor?
34 How could the inventor get by without earning a salary?
35 What is the symbolic meaning of the story?
36 Did the inventor grow potatoes?
37 What do you know about the author of this story, Peter Bichsel?
38 Why are there traffic lights in towns?
39 Why did the inventor often tear up his plans?
40 If the inventor was an animal, what sort of animal would he be?
41 Is this a children's story?
42 Do you think the person who told us the story liked it?
43 What was the weather like when the inventor went to town?
44 What year was the inventor born in?
45 Do you like listening to stupid stories in foreign languages?
46 Was the inventor wearing a tie on the day he went into town or his usual pyjamas?
47 Do you like answering comprehension questions?
48 What did he say to the people he met in the town?
49 How old would the inventor be if he were alive now?
50 Which is the most senseless question in the above list?

Preparation of this kind of questionnaire for subsequent classes

You will notice that the 50 questions given fall into several categories. For example questions 4, 12, 25 and 42 are all to do with the reactions to the story of people the student knows. How many other categories are there for you?

It is vital that you write very varied questions, so that students end up by crossing out very different things.

Below you will find a second story, with a rather different selection of questions:

King Caliban

Fred, huge, strong, gentle but rather slow
Earned £80 a week in shop
Happy: kids, garden; wife Doreen, ambitious, unsatisfied

Fred met wrestling promoter in pub
Offered £800 a week as 'fighter'—all fights fixed
Fred unsure, dislikes violence
Doreen pushes him

Fred becomes King Caliban, paired with Billy the Crusher
In rehearsal Fred slow, makes mistakes, works hard

Town Hall, Saturday night
Audience out for blood
Bald man out for Caliban
Screams at him
Fred nervous, makes mistake hurts Billy
Fight in earnest, Baldy goes mad
Fred knocks Billy unconscious, Baldy screams abuse
Fred lumbers out of ring, picks Baldy up and smashes
  him onto seats
Ambulance, police—Fred is charged

(after John Wain, *Death of the Hind Legs and Other Stories*)

QUESTIONS

1   How old was Fred?
2   Why did Fred marry Doreen?
3   What sort of car did Doreen want?
4   Do you think ....in the group liked this story?
5   Should shop assistants live in nice houses?

6   How tall was the wrestling promoter's sister?
7   If Fred had been to a better school, would he have been happier?
8   Was the story well told?
9   How many fights had Fred had before the Town Hall fight?
10 Is wrestling good for the spectators?
11 What was Fred's mistake?
12 Have you got a brother? Would he like this story?
13 Should women wrestle?
14 What sort of shop did Fred and Doreen work in?
15 How did Fred entertain his children?
16 Who is the villain of the story?
17 Who was the original Caliban?
18 Why didn't Fred like violence?
19 Do you think the writer of the story was an educated man?
20 How many people wanted Fred to win?
21 How much more would Fred have made as a wrestler than as a shop worker?
22 Does Doreen like wrestling?
23 Did the story take place in Manchester or London?
24 What happened to Fred in the police station?
25 Did .... in this group like the story?
26 How did Fred spend his Saturday mornings?
27 Were there more men than women in the audience?
28 Would the story make a good film?
29 If so, which actor should take the part of Fred?
30 Did the story make you feel guilty?
31 What happened to Baldy after Fred threw him?
32 In Fred's shoes, what would you have done about Baldy?
33 Who does Doreen blame?
34 Which is more honest, wrestling or education?
35 If Fred hadn't made a mistake, who would have won the fight?
36 How much money was the referee paid?
37 Was 20% a reasonable sum for the wrestling promoter to receive?
38 How did Doreen vote in the last election?
39 Spell *wrestling*.
40 Is it usual to find gentle fighters?
41 If you cross out all these questions, what will happen?
42 Do you think the storyteller understood the story?
43 Should everybody have the same wage?
44 What punishment did Fred receive from the courts?
45 How many crimes did Fred commit?

46 If your son wanted to be a wrestler, would you let him?
47 Was the Town Hall the right place for a wrestling match?
48 Who is the best wrestler in this room?
49 How long did the story take to tell?
50 What might you have been doing instead of listening to the
     story?

2.2 Theme pictures

Skeleton

Kacuy

She lived with brother in cottage in forest
Did cooking, cleaning; he hunted
She was unhappy; cottage too small, isolated
One day he brought home animal:
She said: 'Cook it yourself.' He said nothing

He knew she loved honey
Next day came home, told her about huge bees-
     nest up tree
Asked her to help him get honey—she refused
'If I go alone I'll spill the honey'
She agreed to help

He took hood and machete, they set off
Finally came to tall tree in clearing
She climbed ahead of him, wearing hood
Near top he whispered 'Ssh, stop or the bees'll hear'
He went down tree, lopped off branches above head
Left clearing, thought: 'Now she will see she needs me'

Cold, night falling, she was terrified, wind rising
Began to grope her way down tree
Her foot slipped into space
Took off hood, looked down: no branches
Her arm itched, looked down: feathers
Felt back of head: something growing
Her feet on branch: claws
Gust of wind knocked her off tree
She was flying; called out brother's name, heard 'Kacuy,
Kacuy'

Ever since Kacuy bird has been searching forest for
  brother

(after Kacuy, in *South American
Fairy Tales*, ed. John Meehan)

Before class

Collect a lot of magazine pictures and details, cut out from magazine
pictures (these should come in useful for a whole range of exercises).
Choose some pictures that, for you, are connected with the themes of
the story and plenty of others that appear to you to be unconnected.
Pictures with the following features might appear to connect easily
with *Kacuy* and its themes: orphans / feathers / lone trees /
birds / families / him–her scenes / sex-role images /
sadness / anger / 'I'll teach you a lesson' / magic trans-
formations / flying / honey = thirst for love / marriage etc.
Choosing pictures that do *not* seem to you to connect to the themes
you can see is important, as people see different things in a story.

In class

1 Tell the class the story.
2 Spread the pictures and picture fragments on a table at one end of
  the room. Ask students to pick pictures that they associate with
  the story. Ask them to pair off and explain their choice of picture
  to another person.
3 Ask the students to find a new partner. Continue this until each
  has spoken with four others.

RATIONALE   The reason for proposing picture association is that
each *listener* creates a story very much of his or her own. Explaining
picture associations to a partner allows the individual student to
realise how special and personal the story he or she heard or internally
created is, by discovering how differently other people saw the story.
Picture association draws out things often otherwise unsaid.

2.3   For beginners

Skeleton

Mrs Peters

Mrs Peters was 80 and leant on a stick
I used to carry her basket back from the shop
One day she showed me a bottle she had bought
The label said: 'One sip of this will take 20 years
    off your life'
She hobbled up the steps into her house

Next time I saw her she was walking ram-rod
    straight. Her stick was gone. She waved to me

That Sunday I went for a stroll in the park
Mrs Peters was sitting on bench near the gate
    wearing an elegant dress and scarf
She looked about 40

The following week I met her in the park again
She was dressed in tight jeans and a sweater
I sat down next to her and took her hand
I asked her to the cinema
She said she wanted to go and change. She said she'd
    meet me in the park in an hour's time.

I came back in an hour—nobody there.
I went to her house and hammered on the door.
No answer

(we learnt this story from a telling by Jan Aspeslagh)

What sort of complete beginners?

You can usefully tell stories to *complete* beginners if their mother
languages are reasonably close to the target language. If you are
teaching English to Dutch, German, Scandinavian (barring Finnish)
speakers and to a lesser extent French, Spanish, Italian speakers then
storytelling at zero-start level can be useful. It is not much use to try
storytelling to Arabic or Japanese-speaking complete beginners.

Before class

1 Read the skeleton very carefully and decide how to get certain words across with mime and drawing. From the above story you can get across the idea of leaning on a stick, carrying bags, hobbling, walking straight, waving etc., by miming. Label, bottle, steps, bench can all be very simply drawn. If you have never told a story to complete beginners before, rehearse the story to yourself, using mime. If all your students have the same mother-tongue, you may find you can translate the odd word or idea.
2 Photocopy the split sentences below, one set to every four students. Cut the pages up so you end up with 16 half sentences from each, which can be stored in envelopes. In writing your own split sentences for other stories, make sure you cover all the key movements in the narration. If you can't, the story is probably too complex anyway. More than about eight sentences can feel overwhelming to the complete beginner. In writing your own split sentences punctuate clearly as punctuation and lack of it are major re-combination and sequencing markers.

In class

1 Tell the story, slowly, measuredly, using mime and plenty of eye contact. In no way will everybody 'understand' everything the first time. Do not feel bad at this 'incomprehension' – there has to be plenty of it on the way to piecing together even partial comprehension.
2 Group the students in fours. Give each a set of split sentences. Ask them to join the halves up and sequence them. Every now and then move a person from his or her group to the next group. Go round answering questions and helping *where necessary*.
3 Tell the story again, still miming and being very explicit. Let them look through their sequencing again.
4 Tell the story a third time, with less mime and slightly faster.

THE SPLIT SENTENCES

Mrs Peters leant	on a stick.
One day she	showed me a bottle.
'One sip of this drink	will take 20 years off your life.'
Her stick was gone and she waved	to me.

She was wearing an elegant	dress and she looked about 40.
I sat down next to	her and took her hand.
I asked her to	come with me to the cinema.
I hammered on the door of her	house but there was no answer.

VARIATION

Old Maid This is a good story follow-up activity at post-beginner level.

Before class

Take eight split sentences and put each half sentence on a playing card sized piece of paper or cardboard. e.g.:

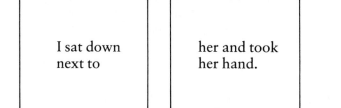

You will need one pack of 16 cards for every four people in your class, so for a group of 20 you will need five packs.

In class

1 Group the students in fours. Give out a pack to each foursome and ask one student to shuffle and deal the cards.

2 Explain the rules:
Aim of game – to lay down as many complete sentences as you can.
Players must not show their hands to one another.
Player A starts the game by randomly picking a card from Player B's hand. A then lays down any complete sentences he or she can. B then repeats the process, taking a card from C etc.
The group sequences the completed sentences once they are all on the table.
The exercise can be made harder by splitting the sentences into three bits each or by including more sentences.

22

Old Maid can well be used for revision of some of the language in a story weeks after meeting it.

LEVEL   The principle exemplified in this unit of making a very difficult chunk of language gradually more and more accessible to complete beginners by mime, drawing and then a co-operative or competitive reading task, followed by further tellings, can well be applied to other levels of learner. So, for example, you could tell a group of elementary students a story that would only be readily understood by upper-intermediates. This is very useful psychologically as the elementary learner is thus having his self-expectations raised beyond their normal level. It is wonderful to end up pretty well understanding something one at first felt confident one would *not* understand.

2.4   Taking roles

Skeleton

The bear that wasn't

Bear saw geese flying South, leaves fluttering down
Said to himself 'It's time to sleep'
Went to cave, piled up leaves: soon asleep
October
In December men came, built factory over cave
March
Bear woke up, went to cave mouth: no grass, no trees, chimneys
Thought it was a dream, pinched himself, no change

Foreman 'Why aren't you working?'
'But I'm a bear'
'No, you're not. You're a silly man who needs a shave and wears a fur coat'
Foreman took bear to General Manager: little man, big desk, bald
Foreman reports; manager to bear: 'You're a silly man who ...'
'I'm going to prove to you that you're *not* a bear'

All drove to zoo in manager's Cadillac
Little bears in cage—manager asked 'Is he a bear?'
Little bears laughed 'If he *was* a bear, he'd be inside
    the cage with us'
Bear depressed
They went to circus: same thing with bears on funny bikes
Bear more depressed
Back to factory, bear worked on machine
October
Oil crisis, factory closed, men back to families
Bear in wood: saw geese, leaves – said to himself
'It's time to ... no ... I'm a silly man who needs a ...'
Colder and colder; white stuff fell, snow
Walked to cave, went in, piled up leaves, went to sleep
    saying
'I'm *not* a man, I'm a *bear*'

(after Tashlin)

In class

1 Tell the story.
2 Group the students in eights. Write up the following eight roles on the board:

zoo bear	Cadillac
foreman	cave
wild goose	manager
Bear	fluttering leaf

3 Explain to the students that each of them is a film director who has to cast the eight roles. Each person must cast the eight roles within his or her group, allotting a role to himself or herself too.
4 Ask the students to work individually, without communicating their decisions to anyone else.
5 When this has been done, ask each person to work with *one* partner to explain how they cast the roles. Do not allow the students to group into threes and fours, which will happen unless you expressly stop it.
6 When two partners have finished talking ask them each to find a new partner.
7 Only after some time allow groups of more than two to form. It is easier to discuss intimate things with one other than with a group.

NOTES   This is a rather intimate exercise that should not be attempted until people know each other fairly well. There are some groups where there is not enough mutual trust for it to be attempted at all. If you try it too soon it may get done skittishly and superficially.

There is no way of knowing in advance which roles will be seen as negative by students. Cadillac, from the set above, has been seen by one person in a group as an insult and by another in the same group as a fair compliment.

Very often inanimate and animal roles are richer than human ones, despite the students' initial wonderment at this novel form of lunacy!

ACKNOWLEDGEMENT   The idea of role allocation we learnt from Bernard Dufeu who had worked with it in the context of psycho-drama.

2.5   Theme words

Skeleton

Jack and the beanstalk

Jack lived with mother in cottage, very poor
She sent him to sell cow
He met butcher – sold cow for beans
Mother angry – threw beans out of window

Next morning Jack's room dark. Beanstalk rising to sky ·
He climbed to top – strange land
Met woman – she said land belonged to giant. Giant had
    killed his father and stolen his money
Jack walked, night fell, came to castle
Giant's wife unwillingly took him in, fed him, hid him in
    oven
Giant returned, sniffed round kitchen

'Fee, fi, foh, fum
I smell the blood of an Englishman
Be he alive or be he dead
I'll grind his bones to make my bread'

Giant ate huge supper, called for his hen, roared: 'Lay!'
She laid 12 eggs. Giant went to sleep, snores shook castle
Jack stole hen, ran to beanstalk, back home
He and mother rich

Jack back up beanstalk – disguised
Taken in again by giant's wife – hidden in cupboard
Giant returned: 'Fee fi ...' Huge supper, counts money,
   snores
Jack steals money, back down beanstalk
Builds mother new house
New disguise – back up beanstalk
Taken in by wife, hidden in wash-tub
'Fee, fi...' Huge supper, giant calls for harp: 'Play!'
Harp plays, giant snores
Jack grabs harp, harp cries 'Master, Master!'
Giant wakes – chases Jack
Jack fast down beanstalk, giant close behind
Calls 'Mother, Mother, the axe!'
Chops down beanstalk – kills giant

In class

1 Tell the story as fully as you can.
2 Write up the words below on the board and ask the students,
   working individually, to put the ideas they find most relevant to
   the story first and the least relevant last. Be ready to explain
   unknown words.

3 Pair the students and ask them to justify their ranking to their
   partner. Get them to re-pair two or three times. These explanations
   re-cycle much of the language heard in the story without making
   the students retell the story to a person who has just heard the
   self-same story.

2.6 Discussion

Skeleton

Peacocks

Peacocks
In park in town centre
Dozens of magnificent peacocks
One day 10 peacocks found dead
Next day another 10
Outrage. Police investigate
No clues
Inspector interviews all peacock fanciers

Meets old man who once bred peacocks
Alone, house neat, military souvenirs, old soldier
He cannot help but be interested in case, pleased to talk
Leaving, Inspector sees photograph of young man in
    uniform
'Your son?'
'Myself when I served the Emperor'

Next day old man comes to police station
Case fascinates him
'To kill a peacock is the perfect act, for a peacock is itself
    perfection'

Night after night police in wait outside park
At last Inspector sees figures approaching: man with three
    huge dogs
Man cuts fence – dogs attack peacocks
Man runs off
Face caught in light of streetlamp

Inspector recognises face of young man in photograph

(after Yukio Mishima)

In class

1 Tell the students the story.
2 Allow two to three minutes reflection time after telling, then ask
   the students to discuss their interpretations of the story in groups
   of three to five (see examples below).

EXAMPLES   In a lower-intermediate group in which the above story was told, almost every student had a different interpretation, including:

1 Rosa thought it was a problem of identification around the photo and the young man with the dogs: perhaps the killer *was* the old man's son.
2 Yannick saw the story as a version of Jekyll and Hyde.
3 Hans (who had also seen a film based on the story) thought that in murdering the peacocks the old man was rediscovering his youth, which for him had been destroying things and people in the war.
4 Christof felt there was no real feeling of time in the story or that there was 'time crossing' – the time of the photo and the time of the killing of the peacocks were blurred or the same.
5 Umberto thought that the old man had discovered who the peacock killer was and had photographed him: he had the photograph in his house because he identified with the young man in the act of killing the peacocks.

NOTES   For this very open, direct exercise to be effective, the story chosen should be capable of a very wide range of interpretation, and the telling should be clear and simple: i.e. the complexity should lie in the story rather than in the language.

Here is another story:

Freyfaxi

Hrafnkel was priest of god Frey
Owned sheep, herd of mares and fine stallion
Dedicated stallion to the god: called him Freyfaxi
Swore only he should ride Freyfaxi

Einar came to work as shepherd
Einar promised not to ride Freyfaxi

Einar lived in hut at head of valley
One day 30 sheep gone – searched – could not find them
Decided to ride out after them
Went to catch a mare – all ran off
Freyfaxi stood waiting
Dare he ride the horse?
Mounted. Rode Freyfaxi all over mountains – no sheep
Returned to hut – sheep there bleating
Unsaddled Freyfaxi
Horse galloped straight off to Hrafnkel's farm

Hrafnkel understood – horse hard ridden
Set off for Einar's hut
'Did you ride Freyfaxi?'
'I did'
Hrafnkel raised axe
Einar stood – did not run – did not defend himself
Without malice, Hrafnkel killed Einar

(from the Icelandic)

2.7   Shapes and characters

Skeleton

Rumpelstiltskin

Poor miller. Beautiful daughter
He told king 'She can spin straw into gold'

King locked her up with spindle and straw
If no gold by morning: death
She wept
Door opened: Funny little man said
'What will you give me if I spin the straw into gold?'
'My necklace'
Whirr, whirr – gold

Next night king locked her in larger room – more straw
(same sequence as above with *ring* instead of necklace)

Third night king promised marriage if she'd spin the straw
  to gold
(same sequence as above with *first-born child* instead of
  ring)

Wedding

One year later – child – She had forgotten little man
He appeared 'Give me your child'
She offered riches, he refused – gave her three days to find
  his name
She sent out messengers to find names
She listed them to him: none right
Did same on second day: none right

Third day messenger reported little man in wood singing:
'This guessing game she'll never win, Rumpelstiltskin is
    my name'
She told the little man his name

Rage – 'A witch has told you, a witch has told you!'

He vanishes

In class

1 Tell the story.
2 Give the students the geometric shapes and adjectives below and
   ask them to work on their own. They are to decide
   a) which shapes represent which characters: miller, king,
      daughter, Rumpelstiltskin, baby.
   b) which adjectives go with which character.
   Encourage them to use dictionaries, to ask their neighbours or ask
   you if they do not know the meaning of some of the listed adjectives.
3 Pair the students and get them to explain their choices to each
   other.

SHAPES AND ADJECTIVES

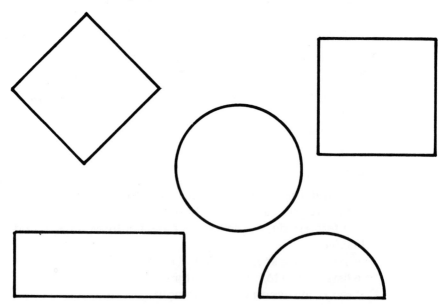

innocent	helpful	astonished
boastful	poor	stupid
greedy	childless	worried
scared	surprised	cruel
kind	ridiculous	desperate
beautiful	terrified	little
strange	amazed	tearful
rich	regal	queer
badly-dressed	sleepless	polite
hard-working	motherly	angry
over-joyed	unusual	odd
delighted	ambitious	empty-handed
pregnant	cross	enigmatic

ACKNOWLEDGEMENT   Lou Spaventa and Gertrude Moskowitz stand behind this exercise. (*Caring and Sharing in the Foreign Language Classroom*, Newbury House, 1978.)

2.8 Completion

Skeleton A

The two sons

Germany – towards end of World War II
A farmer dreams that her son is calling her

Wakes, goes into yard, sees son by pump
But it is *not* her son – one of Russian prisoners of war who work on the farm

The same sequence repeated several times over next weeks
Each time she realises it is the Russian POW

She sees the POWs meeting secretly – they are planning escape
Says nothing – helps them – extra food, blankets

Her son arrives – says Russian army 20 kms away – war is lost
He wears uniform of SS officer

(after Brecht, *Die zwei Söhne)*

Skeleton B

Yvonne

Gloomy town in Amazon forest
Crocodiles in river
Men come to search for gold: gringos
Raven-haired Yvonne in bar, meets men
Leaving bar, many never seen again
20th disappearance
Police from La Paz cross Andes to investigate...

(newspaper account, June 1982)

In class

1 Tell the students one of the stories, breaking off abruptly.
2 Ask the students, in pairs or small groups, to work out endings for the story.
3 If the class is not too large, ask each group to nominate a storyteller to tell the group's proposed ending.

2.9 Story to poem

Skeleton

Willow

In a village – a green willow, centuries old
For the villagers – shade from heat, meeting place
For Heitaro, young farmer, place to sit and think

One day villagers decide to build bridge over river
They come to cut down willow for its wood
Heitaro: 'No, take my trees but spare the willow'
Villagers accept

Next night Heitaro sits under willow – beautiful girl
    appears
They meet, night after night
They marry

Years later
Messengers arrive – announce Emperor wants to build a
   temple
Villagers feel honoured – want to give wood for temple
Offer willow
Heitaro has no trees of his own now – cannot save willow
Thinks 'I will lose the willow – I still have my wife'
Villagers chop down willow

Heitaro's wife is found dead

In class

1 Tell the students the story.
2 Ask them, working alone, to respond to the story with a poem:
   explain that they are not expected to retell the story in poem form.

EXAMPLE   A lower-intermediate student produced this poem:

The Willow Tree

something we must love
a animal?
a house?
a tree?

Heitaro loved a tree
he lived
the love made life
this life was a wife
two children ...
always a tree

The emperor killed the tree
he made a palace
a palace without love is a dead tree
not a house

The tree has died
the wife has died
but not the love of Heitaro

I'm sure that Heitaro,
the wife, the children will live in
a flying house, made of the
leaves of the willow that gets
more each autumn

OTHER STORIES   Any story rich in evocative scenes or actions will serve well for this exercise. Here is another you may like to try:

Skeleton

The singing mushrooms

A widow – three sons: Ogun, Oja and Little Brother
They go off to war. Each promises to kill seven men, take
    seven captives
Ogun and Oja laugh at Little Brother

Each does as promised
Little Brother also kills enemy king and wins treasure
Ogun and Oja angry

On way home pass through desert
Thirsty
Little Brother finds stream
Ogun drinks first, then Oja
Little Brother bends to drink – they cut off his head
Bury him in desert

Brothers
Tell mother Little Brother killed in war
She mourns
Life continues

One day she crosses desert
Sees mushrooms
Picks them – they sing story of Little Brother's death

Return to village – vengeance
Brothers hide in corners of house
They turn to bronze – become household gods

(after 'The Story of the Singing Mushrooms', in *Folk Tales and Fables,* ed. P. Itayemi & P. Gurrey)

2.10   In new clothes

Skeleton

The piper of Rome

Cars everywhere, piazzas, streets, pavements, blind alleys
St Peter's Square – some parked on dome of St Peter's
Mayor – gold chain – called council together
'What can we do? It's impossible'
Council chorused 'It's impossible. What can be done?'

Enter Piper
Offers to free Rome of cars
Mayor offers all the deposits in the banks and daughter's
     hand in marriage
Piper also demands freedom of streets for children to play
     in
Agreed

Piper plays sweetly – everywhere motors start up
Piper leads cars, buses, lorries to remote spot on River
     Tiber
Mayor's car first to plunge into yellow waters
Mayor and councillors cry 'Stop!'
Beg the piper to send their cars underground

And now the cars, buses, lorries in Rome go underground
Children play in the streets and piazzas

(after G. Rodari)

In class

1 Tell the story.
2 Ask the students if they know any stories like this one. Someone in
    the group always knows the original story.
3 Now ask the students to work in pairs, bringing old stories back
    to mind and deciding how to modernise them.
4 Group the students into fours. The pairs report.

NOTE   If you are unfamiliar with the original story, see story on
p.101.

2.11   Birth order

Skeleton

The Billy Goats Gruff

Three goats in mountain valley
Bridge over river – under bridge troll – ate people
Goats wanted to eat grass other side – greener and
  sweeter

One day smallest goat onto bridge, trip-trap, trip-trap
Troll's ugly head appeared
'Who's that trip-trapping over *my* bridge?'
'Only me, the littlest Billy Goat Gruff'
'Then I'm going to eat you up'
'No, don't eat me, eat my brother – he's bigger and fatter
  than me'
'Mmmm, OK, off you go'
Littlest goat crossed bridge, began to eat grass

Next day middle-sized goat trip-trapped onto bridge
(same sequence as above, substituting 'middle-sized')

Biggest goat – long beard, sharp horns
TRAP TRAP TRAP onto bridge
'Who's that trap-trapping over *my* bridge?'
'It's me, the biggest Billy Goat Gruff'
'Then I'm going to eat you up'
'Oh no you're not'
Big goat lowered horns – ran at troll – tossed him into
river

Since then bridge safe to cross

In class

1 Tell the story.
2 Ask who are:
   a) *only* children
   b) firstborns
   c) lastborns
   d) between-borns
   Ask the students to split up into their birth-order groups and discuss
   what it's like being a firstborn, lastborn, etc.

3 Ask people to take a partner from another group and compare experiences.

NOTE   Other stories in this book which are suitable for this exercise are *Three Pigs* and *Kacuy*.

ACKNOWLEDGEMENT   We learnt the birth-order exercise from G. Moskowitz, *Caring and Sharing in the Foreign Language Classroom*, Newbury House, 1978.

2.12 Problem stories

Skeleton A

The two doors

The king never condemned criminals to death – this is
  what he did:
The criminal was led into an arena with 2 doors
Behind one a ravenous tiger
Behind the other a beautiful girl
The man did not know which door was which
Had to choose – be eaten or marry the girl
This was fair – man's fate in his own hands

King had daughter
She fell in love with poor soldier
King furious – young man arrested
In arena he looked up at king and daughter
Princess knew which door was which
What signal did she give her lover?

Skeleton B

Unexpected

Monday:
Teacher says she will spring totally unexpected test any
    day between now and Friday
Students say this is impossible:
If test not given by Thursday, then Friday it will be
    expected
If test not given by Wednesday, on subsequent days it will
    be expected, etc.
Therefore, no way she can spring *unexpected* test

Thursday:
Test comes
Who was right?

(after Watzlawick)

In class

1 Tell one of the stories.
2 Ask the students, working individually, to consider possible
   solutions to the problem.
3 Ask the students to find a partner and discuss their proposals.

2.13 A serial story

Skeleton

The sign of the broken sword

Day one

Where does a wise man hide a pebble? On the beach

General St Clare: successful soldier, had won many battles
Olivier was a great leader and a great general

St Clare attacked Olivier's great army with tiny force
His men outnumbered, many killed, rest taken prisoner

All then set free. Olivier famous for honour and chivalry
But
St Clare found hanged on tree – broken sword round neck

Why?

Day two

Where does a wise man hide a leaf? In the forest

St Clare had committed many crimes in his life
Secretly he had raped, tortured, pillaged
His doctor knew this; blackmailed him
To get money St Clare sold secrets to enemy

His aide discovered this — threatened to expose him
St Clare drove sword into aide's body — point snapped off
Where to hide the broken sword?
Where to hide the body?

St Clare attacked Olivier's great army with tiny force
Men outnumbered, many killed, rest taken prisoner
All then set free
But
Alone with St Clare survivors guess truth
Hang him from tree — broken sword round neck

Where does a wise man hide a pebble? On the beach

(after G.K. Chesterton, *The Innocence of Father Brown*)

In class

1 (Day one) Tell the first part of the story.
2 (Day two) Ask the class to get into small groups. Ask each group
  to work out an explanation and continuation of the story.
3 Ask each group to appoint a storyteller, who will then tell his or
  her group's version of the story to the whole class.
    Get each storyteller to tell his or her group's version to the rest.
4 Tell the second part of the story in the version given in the skeleton
  above.

NOTES AND VARIATIONS

1 If the standard/interest of student storytelling (Day two, 2) is high,
  refrain from telling your version.
2 Instead of telling your version to the whole class tell it to any
  group that may be having difficulty.
3 At all events, try to avoid presenting your version as the 'correct'
  one.

FURTHER WORK   Once the group is familiar with the method used above, it may be developed to deal with longer texts, even of novel length, by spreading the telling over a number of days.

2.14   Story to picture

Before class

Choose an anecdote about yourself that focusses the listener's imagination on a single scene. We used this one:

> I was 9
> Early morning – a fourth floor hotel room in Genoa
> Parents not around
> Went to window, looked down
> Heads and hats scurrying to work
> I spat: hit a bald one
> Drew back – fear, thrill, guilt
> Peeped out again
> Spat
> Again...again...
> I felt fear until we left

In class

1   Tell the class your anecdote.
2   Ask them to draw the scene you evoked, or a previous or later scene in the story.
3   Ask them to compare drawings in small groups.
4   As homework, ask them to prepare to tell anecdotes about themselves. Explain that these should be one-scene anecdotes.

In the next class

5   Get those who have anecdotes ready to tell them to a small group.
6   Ask the listeners to draw the scenes evoked. Let the tellers re-group and listen to each other's stories while this is going on.
7   Using the drawings as a centrepoint, ask the students who were listening to tell the stories they have learnt to others who have not yet heard them.

Section 3   Retelling

3.1   Parallel stories

Skeleton A

Seguin's goat

Mr Seguin lived at foot of mountains
He had had six goats: each had jumped over fence round
    field and run into mountains
Each eaten by wolf

White was Seguin's seventh goat
Tethered her in field
At first she was happy – he moved stake round –
    always fresh grass
He milked her
Told her about other six: how sixth fought all night but still
    died

Few weeks later White became restless
Pulled on rope – kicked at milking time
Seguin asked why
'I hate this stake. I want to go up into the high mountains'
He locked her in shed

Had forgotten window at back open
White leapt out – up into high mountains
Ate new grass, drank from streams, jumped from rock to rock

Sun sank – heard howling in mountains above her
She backed away – could go no further – precipice behind
    her
Grey wolf played with her all night
She remembered the sixth goat – butted and stamped –
    kept wolf off
Sky grew white in East
Wolf sprang – ate her, head first

(after Daudet, *Lettres de mon Moulin*)

Skeleton B

The cat that walked by itself

Once upon a time all animals together in forest: lion, tiger
   etc. *and* cow, dog, goat, cat – all wild
Man lives with Woman and Baby in cave – outside forest
One day dog hungry – nothing to eat in forest – goes
   hunting outside
Comes to Man's cave – smell of meat – warmth of fire
Dog sniffs, comes closer
'Do you want something to eat, Dog?'
Dog shy, but comes closer – man repeats question
Man tempts Dog with meat, then proposes bargain
Man to give Dog food and warmth, Dog to help man hunt
   etc.
Dog agrees
Later, same with Cow – milk etc.
Later, same with Sheep / Goat etc.
Very much later, Cat very, very hungry and thin, comes
   along
Cat sneaks into cave, Man absent, looks for mice, curls up
   near fire, plays with Baby
Man comes back – very angry – throws rocks at Cat
Cat leaves
Later, Woman calls out into darkness
'If you will come around now and again, hunt mice, keep
   Baby amused, I'll let you have scraps, a little warmth –
   but if Man is angry he will throw rocks at you'
Cat agrees.

(after Kipling, *Just So Stories*)

Before class

Tell one of the stories to a tape-recorder. As you tell imagine you
have a real audience, as you would have to do if you were making a
radio recording for transmission. Prepare to tell the other story 'live'.

In class

We suggest two ways of running this exercise.

IN THE LANGUAGE LABORATORY

1 Send out the story you have taped to half the booths. Half the students listen to this in their own time. In the meantime you broadcast the other story to the other half of the group.
2 Ask the students if they want to listen again. As soon as some of them are ready ask them to take off their headphones and pair off with students who listened to the other story. They tell each other their stories.

IN THE CLASSROOM

1 Ask half the class to listen to the tape you have made. Make sure one of them can work the machine.
2 Take the other half of the group to another room, into a corridor or an open space and tell them the other story.
3 Bring these students back and ask them to pair off with members of the other group. The partners tell their respective stories.

NOTE   If you wish to generate discussion after the telling around theme similarities you could brainstorm a theme word such as *Independence* or *Domestication* or *Freedom* prior to the listening work on the stories: a good way of doing this is to ask students to *draw* the first thing that comes into their heads on hearing the theme-word. Discussion of the drawings then naturally provides a starting-point for discussion of the theme.

CHOICE OF STORIES   Stories chosen for this exercise should be parallel either in theme, as above, or in superficial content. The following suggestions may give an idea of the range.
(a) Tell this in parallel with the traditional Goldilocks story (see 4.1).

The three bears

Once upon a time there were three bears:
Great Huge Bear
Middle-sized Bear
Little Small Wee Bear

They make porridge – go out for walk while it cools
Little old woman comes to cottage
She looks through the keyhole
She lifts the latch
Not nice old woman – didn't knock
Three bowls of porridge on table – she tastes them
big bowl too hot – she says a bad word
middle bowl too cold – says bad word
little bowl just right, eats it all, not enough – she says bad
    word
Three chairs – she tries them
big chair too hard – bad word
middle chair too soft – bad word
little chair right – sits, breaks it – bad word
Three beds
same thing
falls asleep in smallest
Bears return
See bowls, see chairs, see beds, see old woman
She wakes – jumps out of window
What happened to her? broke neck? lost in forest? Arrested
    as vagrant?
Bears never saw her again

(after Robert Southey)

(b) Tell 'The river' p.12 (in parallel with 'Two friends' (3.2).
(c) Divide your class into two, three or four groups, then tell two or
more of the following in parallel:

Skeleton A

Jesus was across the river
He heard that Lazarus was ill
He waited two days, then returned to Bethany
Lazarus was dead

He found the house full of people
'If you had been here he wouldn't have died' said Martha

They sent for Lazarus's and Martha's sister Mary
'If you had been here he wouldn't have died' said Mary

Jesus didn't know what to do

And some said
'You made the blind see, why didn't you save Lazarus?'

Jesus went to Lazarus' grave
Asked people to remove the stone
Called
'Lazarus, come forth!'

The dead man walked out of his grave

(*St John's Gospel*)

Skeleton B

He came still wrapped in graveclothes
Staggered, blinked in the light
He stank
People shrank from him
Sisters led him home

Washed him
He still stank

Sisters gave a feast for him
Villagers came
The smell got worse
People unable to look at his face
No one spoke to him

He left the room
Into garden
Moonlight, fresh air

Next morning Martha found him
Hanged on olive tree

(after Hans Daiber, *Argumente für Lazarus*)

Skeleton C

Months later, Lazarus was sitting at home news came:
    Christ arrested in Jerusalem
Mary, Martha plan to go and see him
They expect miracle

Lazarus unwilling
Doesn't feel well
Cold outside: afraid he'll get a chill
hasn't felt too good since ...
... since he was ... 'so ill'

'Lazarus, come with us'
'I will ... only ...

I'm so afraid of dying again'

(after Karek Čapek, Lazarus, *Apocryphal Stories*)

Skeleton D

Jesus looked at Lazarus
Lazarus looked at Jesus
Both smiled

Lazarus went home
Three months later he was married

Jesus stayed by the grave for a few minutes
Spoke about God and eternity
Then left, back across the Jordan

Lazarus was in Jerusalem when Jesus crucified
   the news came: Jesus' grave empty
Lazarus went to see

He looked into the empty grave
And the light went out in his eyes

(after David Kossoff, *The Book of Witnesses*)

Both Čapek and Kossoff are good sources for variant stories. In the area of traditional fairy stories, we recommend Iona and Peter Opie, *The Classic Fairy Tales*, OUP 1974 and Bruno Bettelheim, *The Uses of Enchantment*, Penguin 1978.

3.2 Story-making and retelling

Skeleton

Two friends

During war two friends meet in street
Before they used to fish together every Sunday
Now war has stopped this – battle very close
They drink in cafe – decide to go fishing
Collect tackle – walk into country through own lines
Persuade officer to let them through into no-man's land
Across the river the enemy

Guns start up – they ignore them, begin to fish
They fish, they talk, they fish
Men surround them – the enemy

'What is the password?'
They don't know
They shake hands – are shot

Enemy officer has their fish cooked for his supper

(after Guy de Maupassant)

Before class

Prepare a 'word rose' from the story, e.g.

friends

fishing   no-man's land

persuade   Sunday

supper   officer

In class

1 Give the word rose (on slips of paper or on a blackboard) to half
   the students in the class. Ask them, in pairs or small groups, to
   work out a story from the words supplied.
2 In a separate room or space away from the first group of students,
   tell the story given in the skeleton.
3 Bring the whole class together, and ask students from each half to
   pair off with someone from the other half and exchange stories.

NOTE When preparing your own word roses, you should be careful to choose words that are neither too general to give a clue to the story, nor too specific: 'keywords' tend to rob the exercise of its variety.

By setting the words in a 'rose' you remove the idea of a fixed sequence of ideas, and allow the themes of the story to be seen in greater clarity.

3.3   Fairy stories in the news

Skeleton

Bluebeard

Ugly man, blue beard – rich castle
Has already had seven wives
Marries a young girl

One month later
Gives wife all his keys – she may use all except little key
This opens room in tower
He leaves on business – she explores the castle
Opens room in tower – blood, heads, bodies of seven wives
Terrified – drops key, picks it up, locks door
Key covered in blood – will not wash off

Bluebeard back: she gives him all keys except bloody one
'Where is it?'
She tells him
'Then you must die.'
She begs 15 minutes to pray

Calls to sister standing on battlements
'Anne, sister Anne, what do you see?'
'Only the green grass and the sun shining'
'Anne, sister Anne, ... '
'Only the green grass ... '
'Anne, sister Anne, ... '
'A cloud of dust far away in the distance'
'Anne, sister Anne, ... '
'I see two horsemen coming'

Her brothers arrive – kill Bluebeard

Brothers cleared of murder

Two brothers who killed their sister's husband in a knife fight were found not guilty of his murder at Huddersfield Crown Court yesterday after the prosecution withdrew all charges.

Peter Albert Finniston, 19, a corporal in the Prince of Wales Regiment, and his brother Lewis Finniston, 23, a security guard, had acted in the only way they could to defend their sister, said the judge.

Instructing the jury to find the defendants not guilty, Mr Justice Holmroyd said that but for their intervention Mrs Julie Barber, 19, of Holt Manor Farm, Woodley, would assuredly have been killed by her husband.

Earlier the court was told how Mrs Barber had married local farmer Jacob 'Bluey' Barber, a widower of 53, 'out of friendship' in July last year. 'He was a quiet, gentle man,' said Mrs Barber, 'and I thought he would take care of me after my father died.'

On the afternoon of the 19th October, Mrs Barber was alone in the house while her husband was out on the moors rounding up stray sheep.

She decided to inspect the attics of the 17th-century farmhouse and took the key from a ring in the kitchen. 'He always kept the attics locked and wouldn't let no body in them. He was strange that way,' said Mrs Barber.

Later, when her husband returned and found the key missing, Mrs Barber told him what she had done. 'He picked up the kitchen knife and came at me like a mad thing. If my brothers hadn't arrived, he'd have done me in.'

Giving evidence, Mr Peter Finniston described how he had been home on leave from the Army, and had decided to ride over to Woodley to visit his sister.

'We heard the screams as we came into the yard. When we got to the back door we saw Bluey bending over Julie with a knife in his hand. I kicked down the door and grabbed him while Lewis tried to get the knife off him. Somehow the knife must have gone into him.'

Superintendant Roderick Grimstone, of West Yorkshire Police, refused to comment to reporters about persistent rumours in the district that human remains had been found in the attic of Holt Manor Farm. 'We are still making enquiries into the matter,' he said.

(South Pennines Recorder 21/11/82)

Before class

Prepare sufficient copies of the newspaper item for one quarter of the class.

In class

1 Divide the class into two groups.
2 Ask the students in one group to form pairs.
3 To each pair, give one copy of the newspaper article. (Students co-operate more closely when working from the same copy.)
4 Ask each pair to list on a piece of paper the main factual items in the article.
5 Take the other group away to a quiet place and tell them the story outlined in the skeleton.
6 Ask the students in this group to form pairs, and to work out in each pair how to tell the story to the students who have not heard the story.
7 Bring the class back together and ask each student to team up with one from the other group.
8 Ask the students in each new pair to exchange stories and facts.

VARIATION   An alternative way to use this material is to treat the article as a normal comprehension passage – use any method of presenting the passage that is within their expectations. Don't tell them that the article is only a simulated piece.

Then ask the class, in small groups, to discuss the article to find out if it reminds them of any traditional story they have read or heard.

Finally, tell them how the article was composed – and tell the story.

As a further exercise, in a later meeting, the class might like to compose their own 'newspaper items' from traditional stories.

CHOICE OF STORIES/ARTICLES   If you wish to create your own materials, you can work either from story to article, or the other way round. In the following example, we took a newspaper article and produced a story from it:

The state of mind of a mouse

Bloxwich pet-shop owner Gurmit Singh walked free from Walsall Magistrates' Court yesterday because two veterinary surgeons could not agree over a mouse's state of mind.

Mr Singh, 53, a dealer in rare animals for over twenty years, had been brought to court by the RSPCA for inflicting unnecessary suffering on the mouse by putting it in a python's cage.

He explained to the court that he had been very worried about the python's state of health. It had refused all food for over a week, and had even failed to respond when a dead mouse was put in the cage.

In desperation, he said, his daughter had tried to tempt the creature's appetite with a live mouse. When this also turned out not to be to its liking, she had removed the mouse, unharmed, after about five minutes.

Local vet Peter Barnwell said that in his opinion the mouse would have been terrified at the very sight of the snake, and should have been removed 'after at most two minutes', but his view was contested by Dr Walter Barnes, senior lecturer in veterinary medicine at Aston University: 'If the mouse had been terrified, it would have made frantic attempts to escape, which it did not.'

The python later died.

The python

Rich merchant lived in palace in Bokhara
Horses, camels, caged birds, fireflies, tanks of exotic fish
20 servants to look after them
Merchant had daughter – wise and gentle
She was very plain – this made him sad – she hid from him
Also collected animals, a mongrel, some sparrows, rat without tail

One morning pedlar came to gate
Laid beautiful box before merchant
Inside – blue, green, gold coils – python with unblinking
    eyes
Merchant asked price – pedlar vanished

Merchant built python gold and ivory cage
Gave python special servant to serve him choicest food
Merchant caressed cool coils

After a week merchant noticed snake's colours less bright
Dismissed servant – prepared python's food himself
Snake would not eat – motionless
Daughter found father weeping – took python to her room
Laid it in wardrobe on her silken clothes – it was light now
One of her pet mice died – gave it to python – no reaction
Offered him live mouse
Mouse paralysed with fear
Python stirred, raised head, eyed shivering mouse
Shuddered – collapsed – died
Enter father – mouse sniffed python – jumped over his
    coils
Father told daughter to pack bags
Told steward to sell animals, house – divide money
    among servants
Father and daughter walked out of city of Bokhara

3.4   In old clothes

Before class

Get hold of a different English language newspaper for each student,
or use a class set of one or more EFL collections of newspaper
articles (e.g. Janice Abbott, *Meet the Press*, CUP 1981).

In class

1 Give out the newspapers or books of articles and ask the students,
   as homework, to select the *saddest* article they can find. Tell them
   to come to the next class ready to tell another person the content
   of the article and why they find it sad.

In the next class

2 Pair the students and ask them to tell each other their stories, and why they find them sad.
3 Ask them to exchange articles with their partners. Then ask each student to go through his or her partner's article, and to write down the five most important words in it, on a sheet of paper.
4 Ask the members of each pair to hand their sheets of paper to the members of another pair.
5 Tell the students to prepare, as homework, to tell a story in the traditional 'Once upon a time...' fairy-tale manner, using the five words they have been given as keywords in their stories.

In the next class

6 Group the class in fours, so that each group of four contains the members of the original pairs involved in step 4 above.
7 Ask each member of the groups in turn to tell his or her fairy tale. After each telling the member who originally wrote the keywords should summarise the article they were taken from.

VARIATION   Instead of asking students to pick the saddest article, ask them to choose the most stupid, the most important, or the least informative article, etc. The idea should always be to get them reading in such a way that they are personally involved and aware.

ACKNOWLEDGEMENT   We learnt the idea of emotional selection of articles from Carlos Maeztu.

Section 4   Before I begin...

4.1   Grammar practice

If you are involved in structure teaching, whether straight or cloaked in 'notions', and wish to move beyond mechanical drilling you might want to try this exercise:

Example structure $X \begin{vmatrix} \text{has} \\ \text{have} \end{vmatrix} \text{been -ing Y}$

(present perfect continuous)

Skeleton

Goldilocks

Little girl goes for walk in woods – mother warns her not to
Comes to house in clearing, knocks – no answer – goes in

Tries three chairs
Big one too hard, middle one rather hard, little one just right
Breaks leg of little chair

Tries three bowls of porridge
Big one too hot, middle one rather hot, little one just right
Eats porridge all up

Tired – goes upstairs – tries three beds
First one too big, middle one rather big, little one just right
Goes to sleep

House belongs to three bears – they tramp back through
   forest
In turn, Father, Mother and Baby Bear look at their chairs
'Who's been sitting on my chair?'
Baby Bear adds: '... and who's broken it?'
They look at bowls and say, in turn
'*Who's* been eating *my* porridge?'
Baby Bear adds: '...and who's eaten it all up?'

They go upstairs and look at beds
'*Who's* been sleeping in *my* bed?'
Baby Bear adds: '...and who's still sleeping there now?'

Goldilocks wakes, jumps up, out of window and home

In class

1 Present and drill or practise the present perfect continuous in your
normal way. Lead into a situation in which one student can
'realistically' say to the class: 'Who's been sitting on my chair /
knee / book?' Get people eating each other's sweets, biscuits etc.
to produce a situation for: 'Who's been eating my chocolate /
polos / jelly-babies.'
2 Tell the story and get the class to chorus the 'Who's been...' bits. A
variation is to split the class into three groups and allot Father
Bear's part to one group, Mother's to the next and Baby Bear's to
the last group. They can be asked to chorus in deep, normal and
squeaky voices.

OTHER STRUCTURES, OTHER STORIES   Plenty of stories use
triple repetition of sequences or sentences as an essential device.
Often a particular grammar structure will naturally occur as part of
the repetition, the repetition being central to the story, and pleasurable.

The two stories below are of this sort:

I wish + v. +ed

Skeleton

Three wishes

A man and his wife – neither rich
They talk of their neighbours – richer than they
'If I had three wishes...' said the wife
'I wish there *were* fairies,' said he

A fairy comes – offers them three wishes – goes
   away
They discuss what to wish for: riches, health, long
   life...
Cannot agree
They go to bed. They will decide next day

Next morning wife lights fire
Says 'I wish I had a yard of black pudding'
Yard of black pudding tumbles down chimney
Husband furious
'I wish it would stick to your nose'
It does – she tries to pull it off – no good
'I wish it were gone'
It goes
They realise what has happened

I'll
I won't + *infinitive*

Skeleton

The three little pigs

A mother pig and three little pigs
She sends them out to build their own houses: but mind
    the wolf!
First pig begs straw off a farmer – builds house of straw
Second pig ... sticks from woodman
Third pig ... bricks from builder
Wolf comes to first pig's house
'Little pig, little pig, let me in'
'No, by the hair on my chinny chin chin,
I won't let you in'
'Then I'll huff and I'll puff and I'll blow the house down'
And he does, and eats the first little pig

Second pig – same

Third pig – same, but wolf cannot
He gets angry, tries to come down chimney
Third pig is waiting with pot of boiling water
End of wolf

4.2 Theme sentences

Skeleton

Brontsha The Silent

Brontsha died silent and unremembered
But in Heaven they knew of him and waited
His trial was prepared in Great Hall of Heaven

Brontsha arrived. Defending angel stood to speak:

'On earth Brontsha never complained
Circumcising knife slipped – he did not cry out
Mother died when he was eight – he said nothing
Stepmother gave him mouldy bread – herself drank coffee
    with cream
Father made him chop wood barefoot in snow
Brontsha never complained
Went to city – found work as porter
Boss said 'I'll pay you next month' – didn't – Brontsha
    showed no anger
Married – wife ran off – Brontsha brought up child

When 40 Brontsha run over by rich man's carriage
In hospital full of groaning people he did not groan. He
    died

No one sad – 10 people waited for his bed, 50 for his place
    in the mortuary

Prosecuting angel stood to speak:
Words dried on his tongue, he sat down

Judge welcomed Brontsha to Heaven:
'What reward do you want – you can have anything'

Brontsha said:
'Your Worship, could I have, each morning, a hot roll with
    butter for my breakfast?'

Judge and angels bowed their heads

They were ashamed to have created such meekness on
    earth

(after I.L. Peretz)

Before I begin...

Before class

Put each of the following sentences on separate cards. You will need a set of cards for every four students in the group.

The <u>poor</u> produce <u>the rich</u>
<u>Beggars</u> can't be <u>choosers</u>
<u>Heaven</u> is <u>tomorrow</u>
<u>Anger</u> begets <u>meekness</u>

In class

1 Group the students in fours.
2 Give each group the first sentence card.
3 Ask the students to discuss the meaning of the sentence as it stands. When discussion runs low on this, ask them to reverse the underlined parts of the sentence, as '<u>The rich</u> produce <u>the poor</u>', then ask them to discuss the reversed sentence.
4 Then give out the second sentence card and repeat. By putting the sentences on cards, you can feed in new themes as and when each group is ready.
5 Tell the story.

CHOICE OF SENTENCES FOR REVERSAL   To lead in to a given story the sentences need to be broadly related to the theme(s) of the story, and semantically and grammatically reversible. They should be simple. Sayings and proverbs are powerful material for this kind of exercise.

VARIATIONS   Further examples of this style of exercise can be found in Frank, Rinvolucri, and Berer, *Challenge to think*, OUP 1982.

ACKNOWLEDGEMENT   We first met the reversal idea in the writing of Edward de Bono, but we suspect it may have an older history.

4.3 A picture starter

Skeleton

Gelert

A man had a favourite dog, Gelert
Dog devoted to man and his infant son
Dog guarded house when man away

One day he goes hunting – leaves dog on guard
Wolves attack house
Dog defends child – kills one wolf – wounds many

Man returns – blood everywhere, cannot find child
Thinks Gelert has killed his son: kills Gelert
Too late – finds son patting dead body of wolf

Before class

Prepare to draw on the blackboard a picture of an Alsatian or other (frightening) dog, or ask a student to do it for you.

In class

1 Put up the picture (or ask your student to draw) on the blackboard. Let the students look at the picture and ask them to share their associations, feelings etc. about the dog.
2 Tell the class that you are going to tell them a story about the picture – invite them to speculate on what form your story will take.
3 Tell the story to the group.
4 Allow a few moments' thought after you have told the story, then invite comment from the group.

NOTE Another story that lends itself to this treatment is:

The pigeon

Patio of small, modern house in Montevideo
Retired official
Sun, white concrete
Pigeon lofts – old man waits – season's first race
He waits – wills his bird to come in first

He sees bird circling overhead – early – a record!?
He *knows* it is his bird
Bird circles – refuses to come down from loft
Late afternoon – sun sinking
Bird has special cylinder on leg. He must stamp cylinder in
    a time clock to prove time
Tries to lure bird down to loft: puts on hat he wears when
    feeding birds
Rattles feeding tins
Whistles – no good

Fetches shotgun
Aims
Shoots down bird – grabs it – feeds cylinder into clock
His first win – surely

He clutches broken bird
Breaks down
'What have I done?'

(after Carlos Martinez Moreno, 'La Paloma')

4.4 Picture rose

Skeleton

The quarryman

The quarryman's work was hard – he wasn't happy

Said: 'If I was rich, I could sleep in a bed with silken
    curtains'
Angel appeared: 'You are rich'
Man *was* rich: slept in bed with silken curtains

King came by – gold carriage – horsemen in front and
    behind

Rich man not happy. He said 'I want to be king'
Angel appeared: 'You are king'
He *was* king

Sun shone down – burnt up grass
King saw sun had more power than him – he was not
    happy etc. ...

A big black cloud came between sun and earth
Sun's rays could not get through – sun was unhappy etc. ...

Cloud shut out the sun – made grass green
Cloud poured down rain on rock – it made no impression
Cloud was not happy ...

Rock stood there – man came with pickaxe and shovel
Hacked stone from the rock
Rock said: 'This man is stronger than I'. Rock not happy
'I want to be the quarryman'
Angel appeared 'You are the quarryman'
He *was* a quarryman, hacking stone from the rock
His work hard – he wondered if he was happy

(after Multatuli, *Max Havelaar*)

Before class

Prepare to draw a number of images suggested by the story (say 4–6 pictures) or arrange for a student to do it for you.

In class

1 Put up the pictures on the blackboard as shown below, e.g.

2 Tell the class that you are going to tell them a story around the pictures on the board – invite them to speculate on what form your story will take.
3 Tell the story to the group.
4 Allow a few moments' thought after you have told the story, then invite comment from the group.

ACKNOWLEDGEMENT   Thanks go to Chris and Kathleen Sion for translating this story out of the original Dutch.

Section 5   Co-operative telling

5.1   Co-operative stories in the language lab

Skeleton

The unicorn

The husband woke up and looked out of the window.
   Describe the husband
He saw a unicorn eating a lily in the garden.
   Describe the garden
He woke his wife up and told her there was a unicorn in the garden eating a lily. She said: 'Don't be silly, there can't be; the unicorn is a mythical beast.'
   Describe the wife
The husband went down to take a closer look at the unicorn, but it had gone. He sat down on a bench near the roses and went to sleep. He had a dream.
   What did he dream?
The wife rang the psychiatrist and the police. She told them her husband was going mad. She asked them to come quickly with a straitjacket.
   Describe the psychiatrist
She told the psychiatrist: 'My husband said he saw a unicorn in the garden eating a lily.' The psychiatrist asked the husband: 'Did you see a unicorn in the garden eating a lily?' To this the husband replied; 'Of course not, the unicorn is a mythical beast.'
   Finish the story

(after Thurber)

(The instructions in italic are to the student.)

Before class

Either put blank tapes on the student machines or rewind all the working tapes, and from the console erase both master and student tracks.

In class

1 Explain any words in the skeleton that the class is unlikely to know.
2 Put the lab into 'broadcast from the console' mode and explain that you are going to tell them a story. At certain points you will pause and ask them to fill in the details, speaking on to their own tapes. Ask them to set their machines to RECORD.
3 Tell the first section of the skeleton above and give them the first instruction. Monitor with ear and eye, and when nearly everybody has finished speaking break in gently with 'May I tell you the next part?' Then repeat the process until the end of the story.
4 Ask the students to wind back their tapes and then to swap booths. Invite them to listen to the tape in the new booth and to note down on a piece of paper three language mistakes they spot.
5 Ask the students to swap booths again, leaving the slips of paper.
6 Repeat steps 4 and 5.
7 Ask the students to return to their original booths and to listen to their own tapes while noting the mistakes noted down by their friends.
8 With earphones off: allow time for questions and comments on the slips.

VARIATION   If you don't want to work in a lab the above exercise can also be done in writing. In this case, the story will have to be *read*:
1 Explain unfamiliar words.
2 Dictate the first sentence and give the first instruction. Move round the class helping and correcting as needed. Then continue with the second sentence, etc.
3 At the end of the exercise, put up the stories round the walls of the room so that students can read each other's work.

NOTES   The best sort of story for this exercise is one that can easily be reduced to five or six sentences / short paragraphs. It should be unfamiliar to the students.

When preparing the story for laboratory use, make sure that at least some of the descriptions by students are of more than just individual characters, like the dream description (above). The following story exemplifies this:

Two brothers

A mother left her two young sons alone in the hut while she went to market.

Describe the hut

When she was away, raiders attacked the village and carried the boys off into slavery.

Describe the leader of the raiders

The boys are sold to different masters, but promise each other that whichever finds freedom first will buy the other. The first son is lucky: he gets a good master and learns a trade. Eventually he buys his freedom.

Describe the first brother's master

The second is sold to a bad master. He becomes ill, and at last becomes his own brother's slave. His brother does not recognise him, and ill-treats him.

Describe the ill-treatment

The slave makes friends with his brother's little daughter. She brings him food from her own plate. He tells her his story.

Tell the story the slave told

The first brother notices his daughter slipping away to the slave quarters.

Finish the story

(after 'The Two Brothers Otete and More', in *Folk Tales and Fables,* ed. P. Itayemi & P. Gurrey)

5.2   Group story

Skeleton

The ghost

A young woman lay on death bed
Told husband not to take other woman after her death
If he did, she would come and haunt him

Husband was faithful for three months
Then met woman, fell in love, got engaged

Every night wife's ghost blamed him for engagement
Told him in detail about his conversations with sweetheart
Ghost described presents he gave her

Young man desperate
Decided to consult sage — sage lived in mountains

Sage said 'Tell your wife that if she answers one question
 you will break off the engagement'

Young man asked what the question was
'Take handful of beans, ask her how many you've got'
'If she doesn't know you will realise she is only in your
 head'

Next night young man told ghost she knew everything
 about him
Ghost: 'Yes, I know you visited a wise man yesterday'
Young man: 'How many beans have I got in this hand?'

There was no ghost there to answer the question

(after Watzlawick)

In class

Invite three students to come out and sit *behind* you, facing the
class. Tell the three that whenever you stop in the telling of the story
you want them to speak about what they can see in their imaginations
at the point reached. During the narration you may feel you want to
replace the original panel of three with another panel. In the skeleton
above stopping places are suggested but you should be aware before
you start telling a story where you are likely to want to stop.

5.3 Dictation

Material

SCHOOLMASTER	HYPNOTISE
BACHELOR	SEVEN ROSES
MOTHER	THROW AWAY
DEATH	IMPROVEMENT
FUNERAL	SUCCESS
OBSESSION	BUTTONHOLE
PSYCHIATRIST	FADED

In class

1 Dictate the words in the list singly and in the order given.
2 Appoint one member of the group as secretary and ask him or her to stand at the blackboard.
3 Ask the other members of the group to read out the words they have written down and to agree on spellings for each: the secretary should write down the agreed spellings, in order, on the blackboard. Allow the students to work out *their* versions before confirming or otherwise.
4 When the whole list is on the blackboard, ask the students, working alone or in small groups, to construct a story from the list, following the order given.
5 Ask the students to share their stories.

Skeleton

If you or your students feel the need for a 'definitive' version, you may like to use this:

The seventh rose

A man, 38, schoolmaster, self-contained
Mother dies
Though he has not realised it, very fond of mother
After funeral, breaks down, cannot cope
Teaching, living – all goes wrong
Obsession, guilt, compulsively talks about mother
Harley St – sees psychiatrist
Psychiatrist hypnotises him
Gives him seven roses – tells him to throw away one every
    day for a week
Each time he throws away flower, guilt will lessen
With seventh rose, problem will have gone
Man goes, does as psychiatrist says (we think) – career
    improves – becomes professor at University
But
In his buttonhole, always, is a faded, weedy flower stalk

(after Ken Whitmore, *The Seventh Rose*)

CHOICE OF MATERIAL   Stories for this exercise should preferably be concentrated, and rich in strong 'content-words'. Here is an alternative:

VILLAGE
EMIGRATE
MARRIAGE
ABSENCE
PREGNANT
SHAME
ATTACK
DESTRUCTION
BIRTH
DEEP WELL
SUICIDE

A 'definitive' version of this might run:

Skeleton

No name woman

Village: poverty, emigration
Before leaving, young men marry
A year after husband left, girl is pregnant
Shame
When birth due villagers gather
Masked figures trample crops, open dykes
Kill animals, burn outhouses
White masks, lanterns, wild hair
Faces stare in at windows
She is silent in house
Villagers break in, smash everything
Smear house with animals' blood
As they leave, take oranges and sugar as blessing
She goes to pigsty (to deceive gods)
Gives birth
Feeds baby
Goes to well
Jumps in with child
What bitterness – so to poison the well

(after Maxine Hong Kingston, *The Woman Warrior*)

5.4   Scene to story

Skeleton

The dragon of Nara

There once lived priest in Nara – ugly, long nose etc.
Everybody made fun of him. Bitter
Decides to play practical joke

He puts up notice by lake
ON MARCH 3 A DRAGON
WILL ASCEND
FROM THIS LAKE
TO
HEAVEN
Villagers read, rumours spread
Fisherman says he saw dragon asleep at bottom of
    lake
Little girl has vision
Others dream of dragon's ascension

March 1
People begin to drift down to lake

March 2
Hundreds of people camped round lake, some from
    far away

March 3
Thousands by lake – priest joins them – they wait, day
    passes
No dragon – priest begins to regret his notice

Suddenly: rain, thunder, lightning
Dragon ascends
Priest is ashamed – confesses
No one believes him

Before class

Internalise the story sequence, and prepare an initial picture in your
mind, for example the first picture below. Your aim should be to
establish a mood within yourself, and hence in the group, rather than
to prepare a structure to impose on the group.

69

In class

1 Bring the group into a half-circle round the blackboard – try throughout the exercise to maintain the blackboard as the group focus, rather than yourself.
2 Begin by drawing a strong central image on the board, to set the scene, e.g.

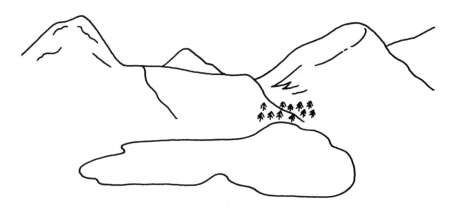

3 Without speaking, invite the group to translate what they see into words: allow as many people to speak as wish to. Do not block any of the suggestions offered.
4 Add a further image to the blackboard scene: try to make the development fit the mood of the students, as expressed in stage 3 above, e.g

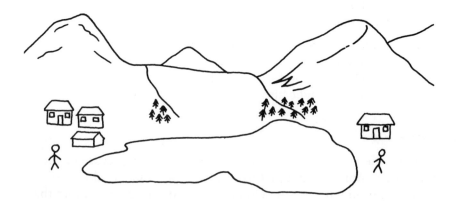

5 Continue, still without speaking, to invite verbal suggestions from the group, then express these in further development of the picture on the blackboard. As the exercise progresses, the story will gradually build up, both on the board and in the minds of the group. Gradually also, to a greater or lesser extent the story will depart from the skeleton given above: this will depend both on the creativity of the students and, in even larger measure, on the willingness of the teacher to interpret their wishes.

6 When the story has reached a natural conclusion, ask the students, working alone, to prepare to retell the story as they understand it. Make it clear that they are free to alter or expand the story as they wish. (As preparation, the 'mumbling exercise' (6.1) may be found useful.)

NOTES   The aim of the exercise is to encourage the co-operative telling of a story – there is no obligation either to follow or to depart from the the 'original' story line, but rather for the teacher to provide a potential frame in which a story can be constructed.

5.5   A story from four words

In class

1 Ask each student to think of a story. Allow three or four minutes for this.
2 Pair the students and ask them to tell each other their stories. Ask them to pick out two keywords from each story.
3 Ask the pairs to take their four keywords and from these build a new story.
4 The students then form new pairs and tell the stories born from the four keywords.

EXAMPLE   In one pair the girl told how a boy had shut her and a girl friend into his car because they wouldn't go along with what he wanted to do. He stood and laughed as they frantically tried to get out of the car. Finally they wound down the window of the car and escaped.

The man student told the story of the two women who came to Solomon claiming they were both mothers of the same baby. He ordered a servant to saw the baby in two. This revealed the true mother: she asked him to give the child to the other woman rather than see it die.

Keywords: ESCAPE   BABY
              CAR   SAW

After some head-scratching this pair decided that SAW symbolised *threat*. The girl then produced this tale:

A couple had wanted a baby for a long time. Finally they had one. Some weeks after its birth threatening letters started to arrive. Desperate to keep the baby safe they one night got into their car and escaped to another town, leaving everything behind them.

ACKNOWLEDGEMENT   We have adapted this technique by H. Augé, M.F. Borot, and M. Vielmas, from *Jeux pour parler, Jeux pour créer* CLE International, 1981.

5.6 Three item stories

In class

1 Give the students these words:
   BIRD   METAL   FIRE
   Tell them these words are keywords in a story you have in your head.
      Tell them their task is to unearth your story by questioning you. You *only* answer Yes or No.
   One story behind the three items is:

   In the dry South African Veld fires are frequently caused when vultures, having landed safely on overhead power lines, try to take off again. Being very heavy birds they can only take off by mighty flapping of their long wings. If a vulture provides a contact between two high tension cables, it is instantly electrocuted and falls to the gound below in a ball of flames. This often starts major veld fires.

2 When the students have half reached your story through their questioning, stop them and ask them to work in pairs making up a story that could have BIRD, METAL and FIRE as keywords. Tell them to make up their story quite freely.
3 Ask the students to re-pair a couple of times and tell their stories to each other.
4 Usually they also want to find out your story; if they ask, tell them.

EXAMPLES   In one group the following stories were produced:

A A man was caught in a forest fire. He was carrying a gold nugget he had found while panning. He had with him a carrier pigeon, so he tied the gold to the leg of the pigeon which carried his wealth to safety.

B A driver of a great truck fell asleep as he drove through the mountains. The truck plunged down a ravine and burst into flames, but he was thrown free.
      When rescuers found him three days later they found he had died of his injuries and been eaten by vultures.

C A parrot in a metal cage saved his owner's life by shrieking in the middle of the night when the house caught fire.

5.7 Random story

In class

1 Tell the class that you are all going to work on stories.
2 Take one student outside and ask him or her what type of story he or she would like to work on. Offer the following well-defined categories of story:
Newspaper crime story
Bible story
Story about unemployment
Football-star story
Fairy story
Let the student choose one category.
3 Leave the student outside the classroom, while you tell the rest of the group that he or she is going to try to discover a story that 'they have decided on'. In fact they are not going to decide on any story but are instead to answer Yes or No to questions, according to whether they end in a monosyllabic or polysyllabic word.
4 Bring the student back into the room. Tell him or her that the group have decided on a story within the category chosen, and that he or she is to discover what the story is by asking yes/no questions. Warn the student that there may be inconsistencies as the group could not agree on every detail.
5 When the questioning has gone on for five or ten minutes ask the group to tell the questioner what has been happening.

VARIATIONS

1 Instead of the rule given in step 3 above, other rules can be used, for example: Is the final sound of the question a vowel or consonant? Does the question contain a particular word (e.g. 'is' or 'are').
2 Instead of using stories, the exercise can be based on dreams: the person coming in is to discover a dream he or she has had, and which the group knows, but which he or she has forgotten. This frame copes better with the inevitable inconsistencies.

ACKNOWLEDGEMENT   We learnt the dream version from Chris Sion. Gisela Mueller had the idea of transferring the idea to a story frame.

5.8 Picture composition

(In this exercise it is intended that the teacher should function as part of the group, i.e. that he or she should participate in the activities.)

In class

1 Draw this on the board, in the top right-hand area:

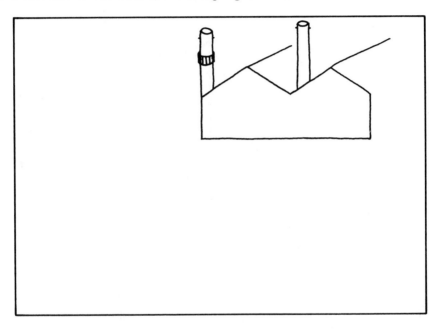

2 Tell students that the group is going to fill out the picture and develop stories from it.
3 Invite students to *say* what they want to add to the picture and then hand them the board marker/chalk and get them to draw in what they have suggested. Add things you feel *you* want to add as a group member.
4 Stop the exercise before the drawing gets too cluttered. Ask people to work individually or in pairs to create stories. (With an odd number of students, you can form part of a pair yourself.)
5 When the group is ready, ask people to form new pairs and tell their stories to each other. Repeat the process twice more.

EXAMPLE

On the next page is shown the picture above after work by one class.

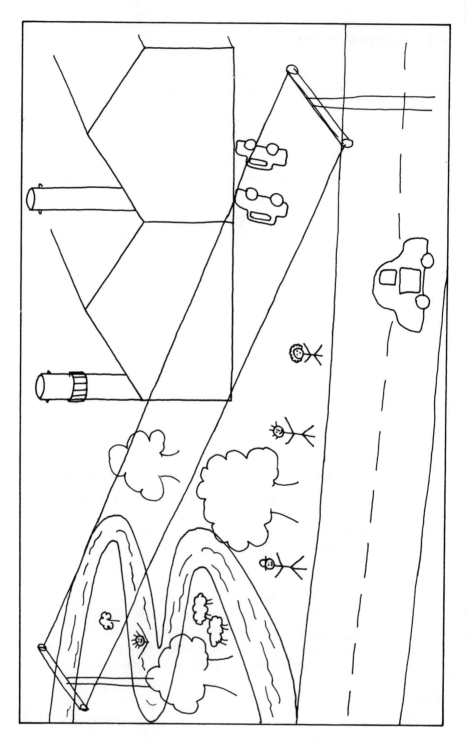

The group produced, among others, the following stories from the picture:

A The three people in the foreground are factory inspectors, who have come to check on workers' complaints about the pollution in the factory. They are so disgusted that they are now going to cross the stream and have their lunch under the tree, away from the filth, among the sheep.

B A great new factory has been built. It is in an ideal situation, near a river, right under power lines with a road running outside the front gate. Mrs Thatcher has come to open it, but because she is very unpopular she is being smuggled into the factory under water, so as to enter by the back door.

C This factory is in Iran and the middle chimney doubles as a minaret. The people in the foreground have just been summoned to midday prayer. Such is their zeal that they pay no attention to their fellow-worker, whom you can see drowning in the polluted stream to the left.

ACKNOWLEDGEMENT   Sarah Braine showed us the power of free picture composition.

5.9   Dictogloss

Stories

A   Solomon's judgement

(Two women had quarrelled over possession of a baby girl and brought their case to the king's court.)
    The king heard their two stories out before ordering his servants to saw the baby in two, which prompted the true mother to cry out: 'No, no! Give her to the other woman!'

B   The forced burglar

(On being questioned by his wife about his frequent absences from the house at night, John thought quickly, then confessed to being a burglar.)
When his wife then started to ask where all the stolen goods were, he was forced actually to become a burglar in order to provide the evidence to support his story, until,

unable to stand the strain any longer, he left home to live with his lover, at which point his wife showed the police everything he had stolen.

In class

1. Tell the group that you are going to read a very short story to
. them once and once only, and that they will have to reconstruct what you have read out: they will be allowed to write during your reading, but there will not be time for them to write everything, i.e. they should focus on keywords and then attempt to reconstruct the rest afterwards. Ban shorthand.
2. Read story A, or an equivalent single-sentence tale. Read at medium-slow pace, but *not* at dictation speed.
3. When you have finished, ask the students to amplify the notes they have made, working in pairs. (If this is the first time they have done the exercise, you might wish to read the story again.)
4. When the students working in pairs seem to have got as far as they can, allow them to mix and help one another.
5. Then appoint one student to act as secretary, and ask him or her to write up the story on the blackboard, taking dictation from the rest of the group.
6. Finally, as a check, give the text to one of the students (not the best) to read to the group.

ACKNOWLEDGEMENT   We learnt this from an account by Diane Fitton of work done at Sydney University by Charles Taylor. The original idea is to be found in an article by O. Ilsen in *Language Learning* 12, 4 (1962).

Section 6   Students' stories

6.1   Mumble, listen, tell

Before class

Get together a wide choice of story skeletons and/or stories. If you
have 20 in the class make sure you have at least 20 stories or skeletons.
Make three or four photocopies of each skeleton, so there is genuinely
plenty of choice.

In class

1 Spread the texts on a flat surface. Ask the students to take any
   story they want and go anywhere in the room they like to read it.
   Explain that they will be asked to tell each other their stories (not
   read them aloud).
      You should move round and very quietly help with unknown
   words. Be available as a whispering reading aid.
2 Tell the students they will be telling each other their stories but
   that first they should 'mumble' the story to themselves, to make
   sure they have got the English the way they want it. A good way
   to mumble is to shut your eyes and say the words quietly to yourself.
3 When the first students have finished mumbling ask them if they
   are ready to tell. Do all this very quietly, so as not to disturb those
   still preparing. When students are ready, pair them off, making
   sure each pair has a different story. Ask them to tell each other
   their stories in low voices or whispering. Go round listening and
   write up sentences you heard going wrong on the blackboard. (It
   is best if, during your writing, the blackboard can be angled away
   from the group.)
4 When the first pairs finish, ask them to set about deciding how
   they would correct the sentences.

6.2 Comprehension questions

In class

1 Give the students the questions below. Ask them to decide on the story they see lying behind the questions. They may do this either individually or in pairs.
2 Ask each student to tell their story to one other person.

QUESTIONS

1 Where was the giant tortoise?
2 What was the boy doing to it?
3 How did the man help the tortoise?
4 What did the tortoise offer to do for the man?
5 How did the man get there?
6 What sort of place was it deep below the sea?
7 What are mermaids?
8 Why was he happy there?
9 Why did he want to go back to the land?
10 What was he given as a farewell present?
11 Where did the tortoise take him back to?
12 What was his village like now?
13 He opened the tiny box – what came out?
14 Why was his face wrinkled?

CHOICE OF STORIES   For this exercise you need to choose stories with a simple structure, the outline of which you can imply fairly clearly with a relatively small number of comprehension questions.

ACKNOWLEDGEMENT   The tortoise story we learnt from a Japanese student. The idea for the technique came from Jean Paul Creton.

6.3 Spoof stories

Before class

Find a smooth, interesting-looking stone to take into class with you.

In class

1 Take out your stone and hold it in your hand so that the group's attention is caught. Calmly and seriously begin to tell the group about the stone. Explain that it is a Cambodian soupstone and that you bought it in an open-air market in Cambodia many years ago. The stone simply needs to be simmered for half an hour very gently to produce the most excellent soup. Explain how you refused to believe this when you acquired the stone but now you have no choice, since you have had so many good soups from it.

   If you tell the story convincingly enough, taking their incredulity as something you expect, some students will want to believe your story. Hand the stone round, let them feel it, lick it and smell it.

2 Now ask the class if they know the word *spoof*. Ask them if they can bring to mind spoof stories they have read in the papers or if they can think of times when they or people they know have tricked others into believing something false or absurd, e.g. around April 1st.

3 Depending how many people come up with spoof, practical joke etc. stories group the students in small groups so that a couple of tellers have a group of listeners.

VARIATION   If the stone story above does not appeal to you, try this newspaper spoof story: 'Last Sunday I read this amazing story in an English newspaper ....'

Skeleton

> British Airways to revolutionise air travel
> London–Sydney: 55 mins
> Passengers will be sent by 30-foot rocket
> Research team in Nakaburo working on pigs, has discovered wonder 'shrinking' drug
> Passengers miniaturised at London Airport regain normal size at Sydney by taking reverser drug
> Scheme not yet perfect because no way to shrink passengers' luggage
>
> (After *Sunday Times* spoof story)

ACKNOWLEDGEMENT   We owe the Cambodian soupstone story to a telling by Carlos Maeztu.

6.4   Story of the film

In class

1 Bring a student to the blackboard as the group's secretary. Get the other students to shout out film titles to him in English. The secretary should write the titles down in disorder all over the board.
2 Ask each student to choose a film he or she has particularly liked and make a poster advertising it.
3 Pair the students and get each person to explain his or her poster and tell the story of the film behind it.

NOTE   It is, of course, possible to dispense with step 2 above and simply ask the students to tell the film stories. We have found, however, that the time spent drawing is pleasurable for the students (as a change of activity) and provides valuable thinking space.

6.5   Love stories

Skeleton

Rapunzel

Man and wife lived in cottage
From bedroom window wife could see lettuces in
    neighbour's garden
She wanted one – man unwilling to steal one – neighbour
    a witch
He finally did – wife delighted
He went again – caught by witch
She made him promise her their first child

Rapunzel born – man gave her to witch
When 12, witch took her to tower in forest – no door
Rapunzel had long, long hair, done in plait
Hung her plait from high window – witch climbed up it in
    morning
Back down again in evening

Prince came, heard Rapunzel singing
Watched witch climb plait
Next day did same
Rapunzel shy – they became friends
He came every day

One day witch found them together
Chopped off Rapunzel's plait – threw Prince from high
window
He fell on thorns – blinded – wandered earth for three
years, begging

Rapunzel escaped tower – wandered everywhere looking
for him
Found him in desert
Wept – tears fell on his eyes
He saw again

They went to his father's palace, married and had many
children

In class

1 Tell the story of Rapunzel.
2 Ask the students to shut their eyes for a couple of minutes and
think back to a love story they know and find important.
3 Ask them to move around and find a partner. They should then
tell their story to their partner.

6.6 From beginnings ...

In class

1 Set a scene ...something like this:
A frog – deep down in a well – lived there since she was a tadpole –
knows every crack and crevice – knows nothing beyond except
patch of light high up above.
One day a quail flies across the patch of light – sets frog
thinking ...
2 Ask students to work on their own, or in groups of two or three to
weave a story from this beginning. If they work alone suggest they
make notes.

3 When students have finished the preparation work (different
people take different times to do this) ask them to shut their eyes
and mumble the story to themselves in English, prior to telling it
to someone else. This produces a much more coherent telling.
4 Ask the students to tell their story to someone they have not
previously worked with.

EXAMPLES   The above beginning prompted some elementary
students towards the stories skeletonised here:

A Pretty frog – climbed out of well – walked and visited all day – at
night afraid – tried to get back to well – lost – spent night in
fear – jumped at a butterfly – but butterfly was hunter of frogs –
ended up in French restaurant.

B Sunny day – frog walking by river – plenty of food – OK. Boy
came to river – water warm – swam – saw frog – caught her.
Took her home to his garden – she was free there – then fell
down well at end of garden.

C Frog happy in wet well – Two children looked down – asked frog
why she liked the dark – frog asked what world up there looked
like – They invited frog up – sun's rays too hot – had to go back
to wetness of well.

CHOICE OF STORY STARTERS   The scene set must imply a
continuation – the symbol of the bird suddenly entering the frog's
confined world does just this.
Here are two other scenes:

Grandpa always in the way – people take his chair opposite the TV
set – no one listens to his views – his daughter-in-law never puts
sugar in his coffee – he has enough of being ignored – one day he
goes to Trafalgar Square...
(after Rodari)

'Here's one that has to be put out of circulation.'
'What's 'is job?'
'MP.'
'You want me to use the three-wheeler?'

(after Vassilis Vassilikos, *Z*)

6.7 ... to endings

In class

1 Dictate the following story ending:

> The woman on his right began to tug, crying: 'Let me go, it's
>   morning.'
> But he refused.
> She turned into a wild cat, bit his hand and ran off into the woods.

2 Ask the students to work on their own, or in groups of two or
three, to make a story that leads to this ending. If they work alone
suggest they take notes.

3 When people have finished the preparation work (different people
take different times to do this) ask them to shut their eyes and
mumble the story to themselves in English. This produces a much
more coherent telling.

4 Ask the students to tell their story to someone they have not yet
worked with.

NOTE   If students ask for the 'original' story, you may like to use
this:

Wild cat

> Scholar and wife lived outside city gate
> Very poor. He studied far into night
> No food for a week – sent her to wood to pick chestnuts
> She came back with seven shrivelled nuts in basket
>
> Suddenly door flew open – woman came in with seven
>   shrivelled nuts in basket
> She looked exactly the same as wife, in every detail
> Two looked at each other
> Both 'Who are you?'
>
> Scholar pulled both to him – gripped each by an arm
> So they sat all night
> Cocks crowed
> The woman on his right began to tug...
>
> (Korean traditional story, collected by Im Bang)

CHOICE OF STORY ENDINGS   Other endings you might like to
try are:

1 ...opened his eyes. Maria still stood beside him, smiling. From the
church on the hill came the sound of bells.

2 ...washed overboard and drowned. But you and I know different.
3 And Peter? Well, he still lives in the village, though no longer in the great house. He keeps the pub now, where the whole story started.
4 The farmer and the cow looked at each other. Then, very slowly, they both began to laugh.

6.8 Objects tell stories

Before class

Choose three objects that do not make an obvious set, e.g. a bra, a light bulb, a kipper.

In class

1 Take in the objects and let the students look at them, pass them round and speculate about them.
2 Ask the students to group in fours and to use the objects as the starting point for a story.
3 When the groups have found their stories, ask each person to work with someone from another group. Ask them to tell the story *as one of the objects*, e.g. 'I'm a light bulb. When I looked down, I...' Do not give time for further preparation of the telling.

NOTE Switching narrative standpoint to that of an object in the story has a powerful 'making new' effect and can considerably modify the story agreed on in the groups of four.

VARIATION If your students already know each other quite well, the following exercise has a more powerful effect:
1 Pair the students.
2 In each pair A names three objects that he or she thinks are typical of B, and B names three objects typical of A.
3 A tells the first part of a story about B, bringing in the three objects. B then finishes the story.
4 B tells the first part of a story about A, which A finishes.

ACKNOWLEDGEMENT   The idea of fitting the story to the person comes from Indian therapy practices, and more recently from the work of Milton Erickson.

6.9   Doodlestrips

Before class

Prepare and duplicate abstract cartoon strips like those illustrated below:

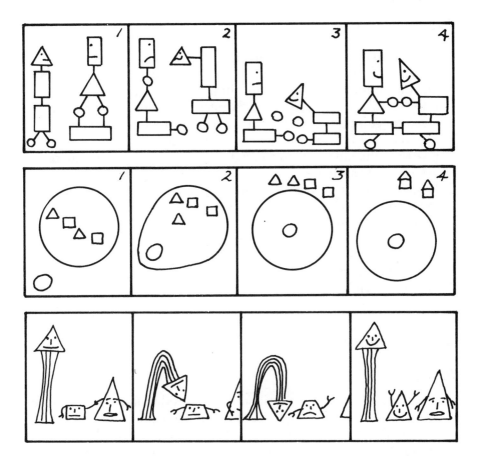

In class

1   Ask the students to work individually or in groups of not more than three.

2 Give out the doodlestrips, one to each individual or group.
3 Ask each individual or group to work out a story suggested by their strip, and to prepare to tell the story to others in the class.
4 Ask the students to circulate and tell each other their stories.

VARIATION   Ask students to 'complete' the strip by adding an extra frame before proceeding to step 3 above.

FOLLOW-UP   When students have worked through such an exercise once or twice, it is a good idea to get them drawing doodlestrips for each other.

NOTES

1 We find that working from abstract drawings such as these produces a very different exercise and group dynamic from work on conventional 'picture compositions'. The latter often lead to rather mechanical, uninvolved storytelling with a high priority given to 'getting the story right'. When abstract rather than concrete pictures are used, students are encouraged not only to give their imaginations free rein, but also to attempt (and succeed at) more adventurous language.
2 When constructing your own doodlestrips, you might find that the most productive method is to illustrate an abstract or very general idea, rather than any particular story-line.

ACKNOWLEDGEMENT   This exercise was suggested by the work of Mo Strangeman (*Magi-pics*, Pilgrims Publications, Canterbury 1982) in the symbolic depiction of fairy stories.

6.10   Triple stories

In class

1 Ask the students each to write three stories that must not be more than five sentences long, the first about a boy and a gun, the second about a teenage girl and a teacher, and the third about a young man and his employer. Ask them to write them on three different pieces of paper.
2 Ask the students to stick their stories up round the walls of the classroom: use one wall for the first story, one for the second and one for the third.

Ask the students to read the stories and to correct any language mistakes they see in any of them.

EXAMPLES   Here are three of the uncorrected boy and gun stories we got from older teenage elementary students.

I know a boy who liked a gun. He got a gun when he was fifteen. He joined a marksmen society. He learnt to shoot with his gun. He was a very good marksman, but he became dangerous and began to kill people.

There was a pleasant boy with his gun in a sitting room. The boy was playing alone because he had no brother or sister. Suddenly he broke a vase and he was very sad.

He was a boy. He want to had a gun. He got a gun-shop and bought a gun. After he got in the wood and shout birds. He was very happy to have a gun now.

VARIATION   You can ask the students to write triple stories about other items/people than those given above, e.g.:

soldier	woman	woman
woman	child	lorry

ACKNOWLEDGEMENT   This idea comes from D.I. Malamud and S. Machover, *Towards Self Understanding*, Charles C. Thomas, Illinois, 1965.

Section 7   From the past

7.1   Photos

Before class

Find a large quantity of old family photographs, preferably not featuring yourself. Try to achieve a wide timespan over the photos. You will need at least one hundred for a group of 25 students.

In class

1 Put the photos out on a flat surface and invite the students to look through them and pick out one photo each that brings back a memory, story, or scene of their own.
2 Ask the students to move around the room and tell each other what their chosen photo evokes.

7.2   Yesterday

In class

1 Draw three scenes on the board in which you were involved yesterday. The worse you draw the better for the exercise, as your bad drawing will make the students more comfortable when they come to draw.
2 Ask the students to make drawings illustrating three moments that spring to mind from yesterday. Ask them to add times.
3 Pair the students so they can explain their drawings. Then ask them to share with their partner all the 'scenes' from yesterday that they care to recall. Explain your own scenes if asked.

NOTES   A kindred exercise is to be found on p.85 of Viola Spolin's *Improvisation for the Theatre*, Pitman, 1964, though her aim is very different from ours. As with many pair exercises, the teacher can choose to take part as a pair member if there is an odd number of students.

7.3   Time-travel mirror

In class

1 Ask a student who likes drawing to come out and draw a large ornate mirror frame on the board. Ask the others to copy the student's mirror onto large sheets of paper.
2 Suggest to the students that these are time-travel mirrors in which each of them can see a scene from his or her past. Ask them to draw the scene.
3 Ask the students to get up and move around. Then ask each person to find a partner, sit down again and explain the story behind the scene they have drawn. Let them re-pair several times. (The point of getting up and moving is that it allows students to choose a partner they want, unobtrusively.)

NOTE   You may reassure students who feel that they cannot draw by telling them that bad drawing improves the exercise; the greater the information gap, the more necessary and productive the oral communication.

EXAMPLES   Here are three or four examples of the sort of things people in one group drew and described.

Elena, a Mexican, drew people sitting round an idyllic place outside Mexico City. She described this very happy period of her life when she was at University.

Marco, from Florence, drew a dramatic scene in front of the goalposts. This was the moment of his first goal for his town's professional under-18 team. This led him on to tell the story of his collar-bone injury that invalided him out of football and condemned him to bored book-keeping.

Nicole, from Geneva, drew a 16th-century lady in a great hall. Her dream, she explained, was to be an observer, an uncommitted person, at the court of Henri IV of France.

Çuneyt, from Istanbul, drew a man fishing in the sea. He then told the story of how his friend taught him to fish in the Sea of Marmara.

VARIATION   Another way of helping students to recall stories/incidents from their own past is to ask the student to draw an empty boxing ring. The students copy the ring and put in it anybody they feel or have felt angry with. They pair off and tell the story/incident/ feelings behind the drawings.

ACKNOWLEDGEMENT   We got the 'empty picture' ideas from S. Striker and E. Kimmel, *The Second Anti-colouring Book*, Scholastic Publications, London 1980.

7.4   It happened to me

Before class

Choose an anecdote area such as 'stupid things I've done'. Prepare an anecdote of your own to tell the class.

In class

1 Tell the class your anecdote.
2 Since listening often starts hares in people's heads, by the end of your telling there are likely to be several people in the group who

want to tell anecdotes of their own. Get them telling their stories to the whole group.

POSSIBLE ANECDOTE AREAS

losing things: documents, passports, handbags, children...
running away: from home, one's job, awkward situations...
near accidents: in the home, on the road...
fear: of things, people, places, imaginary horrors...
if only... stories

7.5 Fire stories

Before class

Get a large picture of a fire or of the results of a fire. It should be in colour if possible. Prepare to tell a fire story of your own.

In class

1 Display your picture – allow time for the students to look at it in silence.
2 Tell your fire story.
3 Invite students to bring to mind fire stories of their own, and to prepare to tell them in English by mumbling them through.
4 Put the students in small groups so the storytellers have listeners.
5 Ask the listeners to tell the stories they have heard to other students.

7.6 Hiding things

Before class

Prepare to tell the students a story from your own experience of people hiding things. For example, my son, when he was six, hid his Christmas presents for the family so securely that even he could not find them on December 24!

In class

1 Tell your story.
2 Ask the students to think of stories of things that got hidden and to prepare to tell them. Discourage them from writing them down. Suggest they mumble their stories through to themselves.
3 Put the students in small groups so that people who have come up with stories can tell them.
4 Ask the listeners to tell the stories they have heard to people from other groups.

7.7 Heroes and heroines

Before class

Prepare to tell the class the story of someone you regard as a hero. This could be someone in your family or among your friends, some local or national figure, or a giant of the past.

In class

1 Tell your story.
2 Ask the class to think of their own hero/heroine stories. It is quite a good idea to allow this to be done as homework, so that students have a chance to get the details right. You should make it clear, however, that they should not produce *written* accounts.
3 Group those who have come up with stories with those who have not.
4 Ask students to tell their stories to the others in their group.
5 Ask those who were only listeners to tell what they have heard to people in the other groups.

EXAMPLE   my grandfather – a miner – during a strike he waited for the police vans to arrive – rolled rocks off a bridge on to the vans – when the strike was over he could not find work in any pit

ACKNOWLEDGEMENT   This idea came from Paul Davis.

7.8   Stories from jobs

Before class

Prepare to tell a story involving an experience at work, either about yourself or about a close friend or relative. With urban, middle-class student groups, stories drawn from experiences as an unskilled worker often have a powerful shock value: they are surprised at the richness of jobs they had considered empty or mindless.

In class

1 Tell your story.
2 Ask the students to respond with job-related stories of their own, or of their friends or relatives.

EXAMPLE   a carpark attendant – sat in hut collecting money – a window on the world – businessmen would linger in their cars before taking them out: the wastepaper bins were full of the girlie magazines they had been reading – rich people would argue fiercely over paying 10p extra if they stayed a few minutes after their first hour – some would sit in their cars for 55 minutes just to get their money's worth – people coming from the divorce court next door would tell him all about their marriages: he was the first human being they met after their divorce

ACKNOWLEDGEMENT   Paul Davis suggested this exercise.

7.9   Shame

Skeleton

The orchard

Boy asks father to take him to work
Father refuses: work too hard
Boy begs, insists
Father agrees

They walk out of town to orchards
Father tells boy to shout if anyone can see him
Climbs over wall and up tree

Father's hand touches apple
'Someone can see you, Father'
'Who?'
'God. What you are doing is shameful.'

(Jordanian story told to us by Lindsay Brown)

In class

1 Tell the story.
2 Ask the students if the story called to mind any situation in which they were involved.
3 Group students in fives to exchange stories, reactions and ideas.

Section 8   Vanishing Stories

In class

1 Write the following story on the board:
'God is everywhere, absolutely everywhere' the little boy was told
by his serious, grey-bearded elders, and so, reaching up on tiptoe,
he grabbed a half-open matchbox from off the mantelpiece,
snapped it shut and cried: 'Got 'im!'
2 Explain to the students that they are going to reduce this sentence
as much as they can. Give them these rules:
(a) You may take one word out.
(b) You may take two consecutive words out.
(c) You may take out three consecutive words.
(d) You must not add anything.
(e) You must not change or modify any words.
(f) You must not *move* any words.
(g) You may delete, change, or delete punctuation as needed.
(h) After each deletion the student who has proposed it must read
the remaining sentence aloud: this must be grammatically
correct and must have *a* meaning, though the meaning may
change as the exercise progresses.
3 As soon as a student suggests a deletion, rub it out at once, without
hesitation. It is the *student* who must justify the deletion, not you.
Often a student who wants to delete a word that makes the
sentence non-grammatical or nonsensical, realises this for himself
or herself in the process of trying to read it aloud. If the resultant
sentence is wrong and the student does not realise it, turn *silently*
to the others and ask their opinion with your face. If no one
realises it is wrong, put back the word(s) deleted without comment.

NOTES   In this exercise there is no need for you to speak at all. You
can demand re-readings or indicate doubt by gesture. This makes the
students concentrate much harder on the board and leaves space for
them to think. Give time for the student you are working with at any
given moment to decide for himself or herself whether the latest
deletion leaves the sentence acceptable or not.
  The group may well be able to reduce the original sentence to one

word (though this should not be an absolute aim), as happened in the example given below.

VARIATION If you have access to an ordinary domestic microcomputer, you may like to write a program to handle the text display and deletion process. A feature of your program, which would be an advantage over blackboard display, could be a sub-routine to recall the various stages of the exercises: detailed grammatical discussion could then be postponed to a more opportune moment.

'God is everywhere,   ' the little boy was told by his serious, grey-bearded elders, and so, reaching up on tiptoe, he grabbed a half-open matchbox from off the mantelpiece, snapped it shut and cried: 'Got 'im!'

'God is everywhere,   ' the little boy was told by his   elders, and so, reaching up on tiptoe, he grabbed a half-open matchbox from off the mantelpiece, snapped it shut and cried: 'Got 'im!'

'God is everywhere,   ' the little boy was told by his   elders, and so, reaching up on tiptoe, he grabbed a half-open matchbox from   the mantelpiece, snapped it shut and cried: 'Got 'im!'

'God is everywhere,   ' the little boy was told   , and so, reaching up on tiptoe, he grabbed a half-open matchbox from   the mantelpiece, snapped it shut and cried: 'Got 'im!'

'God is everywhere,   ' the little boy was told   , and so, reaching up on tiptoe, he grabbed a half-open matchbox
   , snapped it shut and cried: 'Got 'im!'

'God is everywhere,   ' the little boy was told   , and so, reaching up on tiptoe, he grabbed a half-open matchbox
   , snapped it shut   : 'Got 'im!'

'God is   , the   boy was told   , and so, reaching up on tiptoe, he grabbed a half-open matchbox
   , snapped it shut   : 'Got 'im!'

'God is   the   boy was told   , and so, reaching up on tiptoe, he grabbed a half-open matchbox
   , snapped   'Got 'im!'

'God is   the   boy was
told   , and so, reaching up
          he grabbed a half-open matchbox
          , snapped   : 'Got 'im!'
'God is   ' the   boy was
told   , and so, reaching up
             he grabbed a   matchbox
          , snapped   : 'Got 'im!'
'God !'   the   boy was
told   , and so, reaching up
             he grabbed a   matchbox
          , snapped   : 'Got 'im!'
'God!'   the   boy was
told;   reaching up
             , he grabbed a   matchbox
             , snapped   : 'Got 'im!'
'God!'   the   boy was
told;
          he grabbed a   matchbox
snapped   : 'Got 'im!'
'God!'   the   boy was
told;
          he grabbed a   matchbox.
'God   was
told;
          he grabbed a   matchbox.
'God   was

          He grabbed a   matchbox.

          he grabbed a   matchbox.

                              Matchbox!

RATIONALE   This is an excellent exercise to do with tired students
as it requires and gets high concentration. Perhaps this is because so
many skills and operations are happening almost at once:
silent reading for meaning
reading aloud – intonation – rhythm

100

checking inflectional possibilities
checking syntactic possibilities
listening very closely for meaning

CHOICE OF STORY   The story you start out with must be one
sentence and no more. (It sometimes breaks into two or more during
the reduction process.)
Here is an example of a traditional story compressed into one
sentence:

The greedy mayor and bloated aldermen refused to pay the Pied
Piper the gold they had promised him for luring the rats of Hamelin
into the fast-flowing river, which made him so angry that he led
away the children of the city, who vanished for ever into the
mountainside.

ACKNOWLEDGEMENT   We learnt this exercise from our exposure
to Silent Way, though we do not know whether this form of reduction
was invented by Caleb Gattegno, thought up by people round him or
indeed incorporated in Silent Way practice from earlier thinking by
others.

Section 9   Revision

9.1   A story you really liked

In class

When the students have done half a dozen story activities over a period of time, ask which stories they can recall. Ask students each to pick one story they like and come to the next lesson ready to tell it.

In next class

Pair students and ask them to retell the story of their choice. Make sure they do not work with a neighbour who is a habitual partner.

TELL *NOT* REPEAT   In this type of revision exercise the students are not simply repeating a story they have heard or told or both. They are rejecting stories they didn't/don't like and reworking the story of their choice. Providing they have not been asked to do *written* telling of stories, they have no frozen record to refer back to. They have to re-invent the story from the fragments they recall which may well include a mixture of plot strands, memorable sentences and their own reaction at the time of first hearing/telling. As important as all the above is that they tell the story to a person to whom they have not told this story before – stories change a lot in telling them to different audiences.

9.2 Music

In class

When a number of stories have been worked on in class, ask the students, for homework, to choose a story and find a bit of music they feel goes with it. The musical passage, snatch of song, etc. should not be more than two minutes long; ask them to come with a cassette ready at the *start* of the bit chosen.

In next class

Find out how many people have done the homework. Ask one of them to play his or her piece on the class tape-recorder. He or she then tells the story to the whole group. Repeat with other students.

RATIONALE   Even if the student told his or her story to someone when he or she first worked with it, this second telling will be very different from the first. The telling will be affected by the passage of time, by the recall work involved in choosing story A rather than story B, by the thought entailed in choosing the music, and finally by telling the story to an audience under the influence of the music.

NOTE   This exercise may not be feasible if the students are away from their *own* collections of music.

VARIATION   The exercise can be done in the language lab if yours has a group-work facility that allows one student to speak to three or four others and that allows them to listen to his or her machine. In the lab, a student who has brought a cassette plays his or her music to a small group and tells the accompanying story while the same is going on in other groups in different parts of the lab.

9.3 Doodlestrip review

In class

In order to encourage students to recall and retell stories they have heard earlier in their course:
1 Ask the students to think back over the stories they have heard and to draw any images that come to mind.
2 Ask them to choose one image and to develop it as a doodlestrip (see 6.9).
3 Invite them to show each other their strips and to explain how they reflect the story.

In one group, a student produced this strip to convey the story of the Pied Piper (see p.101).

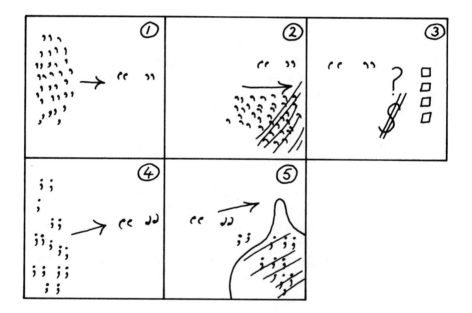

NOTE   Before asking the group to try this exercise, you should have worked through one or more sessions of Doodlestrips (see 6.9).

Section 10 Story pool

A Snow

The typist in the office was happy
'Snow! Snow!'
Everyone except him crowded to the window to see
'All you want is to be on your own.'
But this was not true
Leaving office, he told typist she had a hair on her coat
He didn't go home
He walked through the snow
He went to a bar, had a brandy
Didn't know how to start conversation in bar
Left, walked on through snow
Round a corner he saw man in the shadow, bowler hat
   on head
At first afraid
Then saw other was all alone, like him, in the night
His heart opened to stranger – he told everything bottled
   up for so long
Told everything to snowman with bowler hat

(after Antonis Samarakis, *Zitite Elpis*)

B The pullover

David's gran gave him pullover with flowers on
He hated it
'Lost' it – parents always found it
Left it in garden – dog brought it in
Put it in washing machine on 'Hot' – would not shrink

Out walking one day
Found loose thread in sleeve – pulled it
Crow swooped down – grabbed end of thread
Crow flew into tree – wound pullover off David
Made nest

Next day David showed gran the nest

C   Honour

Teenager lost her job
Father policeman – didn't tell
Left for work each morning
Returned each evening
Several weeks like this
Father asked for rent
She stole
Police investigated
Father had case hushed up
Then he threw her out

(news item)

D   The figtree

Mukami, young, beautiful
Muthoga already has four wives, many children
She falls in love with him
Father against match – says Muthoga beats wives
Reluctantly father agrees

Marry
Other wives jealous – Muthoga beats them – loves her
First year fine
After 2 years Mukami still childless
Husband cools
After three years he beats her – seems to want to kill her

Mukami leaves house
Cannot return to father
Walks into bush – to where dead are buried
Owls, hyenas, wind howls, sky dark
Comes to clearing of holy figtree – belongs to god
   Murungu
Shelters beneath it, sleeps

Dream – god's wife touches her

Wakes – realises she is pregnant, several months
Walks back to husband's house
A cow moos

(after Ngugi wa Thiongo, in *More Modern African Stories*)

E   Ivar

Ivar – great poet of Iceland
Sailed to Norway with brother
King made him court poet
Ivar sent brother back with message for sweetheart
Asked her to wait for him

Sweetheart fell in love with brother
They married

Ivar to Iceland
Discovered truth
Back to Norway
Each day more miserable

King: 'Angry with someone here?' Ivar: 'No'
King: 'More honours?' Ivar: 'No'
King: 'A woman?' 'Yes'
'Shall I send for her?' 'Married'
'Another?' 'No help'
'Then when I am free, you can talk to me of her –
    sadness lessens when you can talk'
'You honour me, my Lord'

(from the Icelandic)

F   In the cellar

Army retreat
Hiding in basement – very tired, no food, dark
Suddenly: TICK-TACK in next cellar
Again
Terror
Gripped machine-gun
Friend with torch
TICK-TACK
Tiptoed to door
TICK-TACK
Burst in

Two fleas on a see-saw in corner

G The donkey

Two thieves see idiot leading donkey along road
Decide to steal it
One slips collar off donkey – takes donkey's place
Other takes donkey, sell in market

After a mile, idiot sees thief in donkey's collar
Thief explains:
Under curse for drinking, beating mother
Now curse lifted – mother must have forgiven
Idiot gives him money – sends him off

Idiot to market to buy new donkey
Recognises old one
'Aha! Been beating your mother again! Shan't buy *you*
again!'

(from *1001 Nights*)

H Oogledeboo

'Make a penny go away, Granddad'
He took penny, blew, it disappeared
'Again'
He did
'How?'
'I say "oogledeboo" and it vanishes'
She tries, it vanishes, Granddad leaves, puzzled

Next day she goes shopping with Mummy
Fat lady in way
'Oogledeboo'
Lady vanishes
Then she vanishes furniture, lift full of people, neighbour's
    son
Parents call doctors, psychiatrists, conjurors...
No effect

One day Granddad comes
Tells her to bring things and people back
'How?'
Must say 'oogledeboo' backwards
She does
Things and people return

She tries to vanish things again
Fails
'Pity, Granddad'

(after Will F. Jenkins, in *Saturday Evening Post Reader*
of *Fantasy and Science Fiction)*

I   The man, the snake, and the stone

Man lifts flat stone by road
Snake comes out – says will kill man
Man begs for one chance
Snake: 'We'll ask next creature we meet to decide'

Meet sheep – against man – mutton
One more chance

Meet horse – against man – slavery
One more chance

Meet fox
Asks them to take him back to stone
Tells snake to lie where he was
Fox replaces stone on snake

Fox asks payment
Go to man's house
Man gives chicken in sack
Says open sack away from house – neighbours won't like
    him helping fox
'Go to that clump of trees, it's quiet there'
Fox goes

Hunters in trees
Shoot fox

Matter settled
And man? His turn still to come

(after Idries Shah, *Caravan of Dreams)*

J   The baby

Village family: 14 children
very poor
father places eldest daughter, 12, in service in town
one less mouth to feed
she works 15-hour day
mistress has baby
she looks after baby while mistress works
half day off per week – gets pregnant
mistress discovers – sacks her
nowhere to go
she meets a pimp...

K   The husband

Cold night
Traveller crossing moor
Knocked on farm door
Woman by corpse – candle light
'He's just died in my arms'
Wept
Asked traveller to watch corpse
Fear
Came back with young man
Gave the two men tea
Young man into bedroom
She too
Corpse opened eyes
Looked at traveller

(after J.M. Synge, *The Aran Islands*)

L   Enkidu

Goddess pictured Enkidu in her mind's eye
Took water, clay – let it fall in desert
Enkidu made

He ran with gazelle – long hair like woman – hair matted
   on body
Trapper's son saw him at water-hole – froze with fear
Told father 'This man is strongest in world – tears up
   my traps. Help me'
Father told him to go to city and get woman

Trapper's son to city
Brought woman to waterhole
They waited there three days

Then Enkidu came with gazelle
Trapper's son to woman: 'show yourself naked, teach him'
She did
Enkidu spent seven nights with her

He went back to gazelle, they bolted, his knees gave way
He came to her
Sat at her feet
Said 'Take me to the city'

(From the *Epic of Gilgamesh*)

M   Ophir

Fifteenth-century Venice
Old man, tattered, dirty, asks to see doge
Tells how he visited fabled land of Ophir
Asks doge for ship to return and bring back treasure

Doge, Bishop question him
Tells them – sailed round Africa
Flew inland on winged horses
People of Ophir traded iron for gold

Shipwreck – treasure lost

Bishop: 'Are there centaurs there?' No
'Birds of bronze with steel beaks?' No
'What trees?' Palms

Bishop says man is liar
There are centaurs, birds of bronze
Trees are pomegranates

Man sold to galleys as slave

(after Karel Čapek, *Apocryphal Stories*)

111

N A horse race

Merchant had two lazy sons
They gambled, raced horses
Left his fortune to *one* of his sons – no division
A horse race to decide who inherits
Son whose horse reaches London Bridge *last* will win

Merchant died
Sons began race
Six months later they had gone two miles
An old man saw them – laughed
'You can end the race today if...'

Advice was?

O The wisdom of the world

Tortoise decides to collect all wisdom in world
Does so
Puts it in gourd and seals it up
Goes to hide it up tree
Puts rope round gourd, hangs it round neck
Starts to climb, finds he cannot
Hunter comes along
'Hang gourd on back'
Tortoise realises he cannot collect *all* wisdom
Throws gourd away
It breaks
Bits fly all over world
You want wisdom?
Go and try to find some of the bits

(after 'Tortoise and the wisdom of the world' in
Folk Tales and Fables, ed. P. Itayemi & P. Gurrey)

P   The princess and the pea

Once a prince
Wanted to marry a princess
But a *real* princess
How to find?

One dark night
Storm rain lightning thunder
Knock on door
King went downstairs, opened up
Outside a princess
Dripping wet
King has idea

Invited her in – food, clean clothes
Bed for night – special bed!
20 mattresses, 20 featherbeds
And under all: one pea

Princess to bed
Not a wink of sleep
Bed too lumpy

Aha! a real princess
Prince fell in love
Married
Happy ever after
And the pea is in the palace still, unless someone has
    walked off with it

So it was a true story

(after H.C. Andersen)

Q   The poem

Great battle – victory
King to poet: 'Celebrate my victory in song'
A year passes – a great poem
King gives poet silver mirror
'Now make a greater poem'

A year passes – second poem is magnificent
Much shorter
King gives poet golden mask
'Now a third – the greatest'

A year passes – poet whispers poem to king
Single line of verse
'True poetry'
King gives poet dagger of iron

Poet leaves palace – kills himself
King leaves palace – a wandering beggar

(after J.L. Borges, *The Mirror and the Mask*)

R   An old man

West of Ireland
Film location
Sea, moorland
Director meets old man – wants him to act in film
'You should see my father'
Father lives in hut by sea
Doesn't speak English
Unbelievably old

Son translates – father agrees to act
Filming takes two weeks
Final scene: old man looks to sea, as family leave for USA
Director whispers to son
Son translates
Retake of scene – same, but old man's eyes turn deepest
   blue with tears

End of film
Photographer takes polaroid of old man
Hands it to him
He looks, snarls, tears up photo
Storms of muttering in Gaelic
The son translates:
'This is a picture of an *old* man'

(after Harry Towb)

S   Ants

I saw a family of red ants – stamped on them
But I had stamped on other children
I walked on
Looked back – ant following me
Saw where I lived

Next day ants big as people came to our house
We ran away
Moved to better house

(Deborah, aged 10)

T The magic barrel

New York student: to become rabbi
Needs wife
Calls matchmaker
Photographs: widow, lame girl, schoolteacher
Agrees to meet teacher
Disaster – he is shy

Matchmaker returns – more photographs
He has a barrel full of them, he says
Student sends him away
Photos left on table – packet with six in colour and one
    in black and white
Black and white photo shows girl with deep eyes, a girl
    who has suffered

He falls in love
Goes to matchmaker's home – bare, no furniture,
    no barrel
'Who is this girl'
Matchmaker turns white: 'my daughter – an error, not
    for you – dead'

Student doesn't believe him – demands to meet her
'She disgraced us'
Insists – meeting under streetlamp
A thin, pale girl, gaudily dressed
Tart?
In the shadows, her father chants prayer for the dead

(after Bernard Malamud, *The Magic Barrel*)

Notes and suggestions

The stories collected in the Story pool are intended as a supplement
to the stories to be found in the body of this book, and as a starting-
point for teachers who want to build up their own storytelling
repertoire. We have, therefore, not provided lesson notes or exercise
materials for them. As an example of how the stories in the pool
might be used, the following is offered as a suggestion:

Story Exercises

A 2.5 (you will need to write your own theme words)
   2.9
   3.1 (parallel with story E)
B 2.3
   2.14 (in place of the anecdote given)
C 2.2
   3.1 (parallel with story J)
   5.3 (you will need to select your own 'content words')
   7.9
D 2.5 (you will need to write your own theme words)
   5.4
E 2.7
   3.1 (parallel with story A)
   3.2 (you will need to construct your own 'word rose')
F 2.8 (e.g. tell as far as penultimate line only)
G 2.10
H 2.4
I 2.2
   2.13 (break at line 13)
   4.2 (try finding your own theme sentences, e.g. 'Death before
        dishonour')
J 3.1 (parallel with story C)
   3.4
K 6.7 (start at e.g. line 11)
L 2.5 (you will need to write your own theme words)
M 2.6
   2.7
   3.2 (you will need to construct your own 'word rose')
N 2.12
O 2.2
P 2.10 (either rewrite the story yourself 'in new clothes' or get
        the class to rework it)

Q   2.6

        2.9

        4.4 (pictures of e.g. crown, mask, dagger, beggar)

R   3.2 (you will need to make your own 'word rose')

        4.2 (you will need to write your own theme sentences)

        6.2 (this story provides a good opportunity to try writing 'comprehension questions' of this sort)

S   2.6

        4.3 (ant)

T   2.1 (either write the questions yourself, or get one class to write the questions for another group)

        2.7

Postscript

Books like this have no real business to finish. The reader could usefully and excitingly go on into the following areas:

1 Guided fantasies. The group leader, after a relaxation exercise, talks the participants through the outline of a fantasy so constructed as to leave the whole filling-out of the situation to the experience and imagination of the listener. A well-conducted guided fantasy leaves the participant more with the sense of having lived through a novel or dream than a short story, though the time of the telling is perhaps no more than five minutes, excluding pauses for inner imaginative work.

2 Recall of buried stories from childhood. Everybody has stories heard in childhood and of great significance then, which resist being dug up. They seem often to surface only in fragments, and areas in and around them are often blocked.

3 Childhood fantasies. The waking dreams people wove for themselves as children, before reaching sleep. They may have been influenced by elements from such sources as adult tellers, TV, radio and books. They may have had to do with areas like fears, omnipotence, sexuality.

4 Dreams. There are a number of non-judgemental, non-analytic ways of working with dreams as stories variously understood by different people in a group. There are, too, the Gestalt techniques for exploring a dream from the point of view of objects and people *within* it.

We have not included exercise material in the above areas because our teaching situation did not allow us to reach the depth of mutual trust required to enter such delicate and fraught territory. People interested in guided fantasies might find these two books of interest:

G. Moskowitz, *Caring and Sharing in the Foreign Language Classroom*, Newbury House, 1978.

John O. Stevens, *Awareness: exploring, experimenting, experiencing*, Real People Press, Utah, 1971.

If you are interested in story work from dreams then Chapter 14 of *Handbook of Dreams*, edited by B.B. Wolman, Van Nostrand Reinhold Co. 1979 may provide a way in.

Acknowledgements

The authors and publishers would like to thank the following publishers and organisations for permission to adapt extracts from published works. As it has not been possible to identify all sources, the publishers will welcome information from copyright holders.

Frederick Muller Ltd for *South American Fairy Tales* on pp. 18–19; Penguin Books Ltd for *Folk Tales and Fables,* eds. P. Itayemi and P. Gurrey on pp. 5, 34, 65, 112, *Cuentos Hispanicos* on p. 60, and *The Epic of Gilgamesh,* trans. N.K. Sanders on pp.110–11; Allen and Unwin for *Apocryphal Stories,* trans. Dora Round on pp. 45–6, 111; *The Pragmatics of Human Communication,* © 1967 by W.W. Norton and Co. Ltd on pp. 38, 65–6; A.P. Watt Ltd for *The Innocence of Father Brown* on pp. 38–9, and *Caravan of Dreams* on p. 109; Fount Paperbacks for *The Book of Witnesses* on p. 46; Random House Inc. and Alfred Knopf Inc. for *Max Havelaar,* trans, and ed. W. Siebenhaar on pp. 60-1; Mrs Helen Thurber for *Fables of our Time* (Harper and Row), © 1940 James Thurber, © 1968 Helen Thurber on p. 53; Mr Ken Whitmore for *The Seventh Rose* on p. 67; Charles E. Tuttle Co. Inc. for *Korean Folk Tales,* ed. Im Bang and Yi Ryuk on p. 85; Fontana Paperbacks for *More Modern African Stories,* ed. C.R. Larson on p. 106; Mr Harry Towb for *The Old Man* on p. 115.
We are grateful to The Central Office of Information for the photograph on p. 94.